Technology and
Economic Development

Technology and Economic Development

Martin Fransman
Lecturer in Economics
University of Edinburgh

WESTVIEW PRESS
Boulder, Colorado

First published in Great Britain in 1986 by
WHEATSHEAF BOOKS LTD
A MEMBER OF THE HARVESTER PRESS PUBLISHING GROUP
Publisher: John Spiers
Director of Publications: Edward Elgar
16 Ship Street, Brighton, Sussex

© Martin Fransman, 1986

ISBN 0–8133–0418–0
LCN 86–50429

Published in 1986 in the United States by
WESTVIEW PRESS
Frederick A. Praeger, Publisher
5500 Central Avenue
Boulder, Colorado 80301

Typeset in 11 on 12 point Times
Printed in Great Britain

For Judith and Karen

Contents

PART II
Directions for Future Research

Preface

In 1982 I was invited by the Editors of the *Journal of Development Studies* to prepare a survey of recent material in the area of technology in less developed countries. Having recently jointly edited *Technological Capability In The Third World* (Macmillan, 1984) which was based on a conference held in Edinburgh in 1982, I had acquired a large number of unpublished papers and reports. To this were added numerous books sent to me by one of the editors of the *Journal* and many other articles and publications. In addition to the quantity of material, I had to take account of conceptual changes that had recently occurred. For a number of reasons (considered in detail in this book) a fundamental change was taking place in the conceptualisation of the process of technical change. This was true both in the rich countries where a revival of neo-Schumpeterian thought was emerging, as well as in the context of less developed countries where the demise of neoclassical economics and rigid versions of dependency theory had opened the door to wider-ranging work on the process of technical change. In the attempt to put all this into perspective, the survey grew and grew and eventually became an 'interpretive survey' which, it is hoped, more or less accurately reflects the flavour of continuity and change in this area of development studies.

While the survey was published by the *Journal of Development Studies* (Vol. 21, No. 4, July 1985) it was decided for two reasons to publish the present book. First, in order to make the survey more widely available, in view of the growing interest from both an academic and a policy point of view in the question of technical change. And second, in order to reflect further on desirable directions for future research in this area. This is done in Part 2, which concentrates on some of the new conceptualisations that are needed if the process of technical change is to be understood. The whole field of technology studies is currently in a state of great flux as new questions begin to be asked and new directions explored. Some of this change is reflected in this Part as an attempt is made to pinpoint some of the areas which require further theoretical and empirical work.

In addition to expressing my gratitude to those mentioned in the Acknowledgements who generously gave of their time and commented (in some cases in great detail) on a first draft of the survey, I would like particularly to acknowledge the intellectual stimulation and constant encouragement received over the last few years from Sanjaya Lall and Norman Clark. In addition, members of the Edinburgh Technology Group, and in particular Donald MacKenzie and Barry Barnes, have opened my eyes to some issues to which many economists remain blind. While errors and deviations remain my own, I have benefited from their discussion. Last, but by no means least, I must acknowledge the support and sacrifice of Tammy, Judith and Karen for whom another deadline has become almost as bad as a dentist appointment.

MARTIN FRANSMAN
Edinburgh, January 1986

Acknowledgements

Part I is reprinted by permission of Frank Cass & Co. Ltd, Publishers.

The author would like to express his gratitude to those who gave generously of their time by reading and commenting on an earlier draft of Part I. These comments were extremely valuable, and working through them provided an important learning experience. While without doubt many ideas remain with which they would not agree, the author would like to thank Ron Dore, Staffan Jacobsson, Raphie Kaplinsky, Sanjaya Lall, Don Mackenzie, Richard Nelson, Gustav Ranis, Nathan Rosenberg, Amartya Sen, Frances Stewart and Larry Westphal. A special acknowledgement is due to David Booth for valuable comments and for assistance in obtaining literature.

Part I
Conceptualising Technical Change in the Third
World in the 1980s: An Interpretive Survey

1 Introduction

Technical change is central to the process of economic development. As defined in this Part, technical change refers to improvements in the transformation of inputs into outputs, including improvements in the quality of output. Such improvements are an integral part of the process of economic growth which in turn is necessary for the broader process of economic development.

However, despite the centrality of technical change, the phenomenon itself is still poorly understood. This emerges as clearly in the literature on the industrialised countries as it does in that pertaining to the Third World. In a book significantly titled *Inside the Black Box: Technology and Economics*, Rosenberg concludes regarding the question 'of the social determinants of a society's capacity for generating technical progress in the first place' that 'on this most fundamental issue, our understanding remains, at best, rudimentary' (Rosenberg, 1982: 29). Similarly, in a major review of work on productivity growth, Nelson (1981) states:

The premise behind this paper is that the theoretical model underlying most research by economists on productivity growth over time, and across countries, is superficial and to some degree even misleading regarding the following matters: the determinants of productivity at the level of the firm and of inter-firm differences; the processes that generate, screen, and spread new technologies; the influence of macroeconomic conditions and economic institutions on productivity growth (p. 1029).

Conclusions such as these are sobering when it is remembered that Chapter One of Adam Smith's *Wealth of Nations* dealt largely with questions of technical change and productivity improvement.

Like technology itself, the conceptual study of technology is not static but continually changes. At some times the change is more rapid than at others. A major theme running through this article deals with changing conceptualisations of the process of technical change. These changes in conceptualisation involve fundamentally different ways of viewing firms and their environments. The changes referred to are reflected clearly in the literature on technical change in the Third World. Previously attention focused largely on the questions of the choice of technique and the cost of transferring foreign technology. More recently the focus has shifted to a consideration of the complex process of technical change in Third World countries. Thus Stewart and James (1982) argue:

In the 1960s and 1970s most research on technology in poor countries was directed at the question of the labour or capital intensity of production technique (sometimes described as the 'neo-classical' question). But recently ... the focus has changed quite radically .... In general, the new perspectives are concerned with technology in a *dynamic* setting, with attention on how technology changes over time, whereas previously the major concern was the *static* question of choice out of a given set of techniques. (p. 1)

Similarly, in a perceptive review, Lall (1981a) concludes that there 'is little doubt that LDC innovation and generation of technology will comprise the main areas of investigation and action [in the technology field in developing countries] in the next decade or so. This will serve to build the missing, but vital, link between the conventional study of technology in industrialised countries and in the Third World' (p. 124).

The changes in the conceptualisation of technical change are considered in more detail particularly in section II, where the technology market and the transfer of technology, and choice of technique and appropriate technology, are discussed, and section IV, where sources of technical change are examined. In section III the definition, forms and measurement of technical change are considered. But why did the approach to technology issues in the Third World change at the time that it did, namely, in the latter 1970s? This question is pursued further in section VI, where it is suggested that the demise of the dependency and neoclassical economics paradigms, and the rise of the newly-industrialised countries, were important influences.

In section V the unique role of the capital goods sector in the generation and diffusion of technical change is examined while in section VII a perennial question in discussions of technology in the Third World, namely, whether developed country technology constitutes on balance an opportunity or a constraint, is re-examined in the light of the new conceptualisations. The role of technical change in the analysis of infant industries and exporting activities (including technology exports) is considered in section VIII and attention is drawn to the divergence between some of the conclusions and policy prescriptions of conventional economic theory and the experience of a newly industrialised country. Section IX then deals with the role of the state in shaping, stimulating and inhibiting various forms of technical change. It is shown that we are still a long way from an adequate explanation of the state's important interventions in the area of technology,

While an overall concern in all of these sections is with alternative conceptualisations of the process and determinants of technical change, equal emphasis is given to the implications for policy-making. Here an underlying theme is the dilemma presented for both analysis and policy by the inherent uncertainty accompanying technical change.

There are, however, a number of omissions in this selective review. Most of the material covered relates to technology in the manufacturing sector and, while the conceptual and theoretical issues remain pertinent, nothing is said about the specific issues that emerge in the primary or service sectors. Furthermore, to the extent that empirical material is examined for particular countries, these tend to be among the more, rather than the less, industrialised. This is an important shortcoming since additional analytical and policy problems will be presented in countries where the technology gap between current practice and the world technology frontier is qualitatively, as well as quantitatively, greater. However, in this connection two points may be made. First, most of the conceptual issues discussed relating to the analysis of technical change will be relevant for countries at lower levels of industrialisation and technological sophistication. Second, the concentration on more industrialised Third World countries may be justified in terms of an analysis of what is possible under the most favourable conditions existing in the Third World. Clearly, however, the additional, and to some extent different, problems confronted in less industrialised countries will be important.[1]

Finally, it should be noted that as far as possible an attempt has been made in this review to summarise and assess the new directions that have emerged in the literature. While at times this has necessitated a consideration of the more established areas from which the new directions have emerged, in general little effort has been made to summarise the consensus and disagreement in these established areas. Wherever possible the reader has been referred to other reviews and articles that cover these areas.

2 New Thinking on Old Themes

THE TECHNOLOGY MARKET AND THE TRANSFER OF TECHNOLOGY[2]

The international 'transfer of technology' refers essentially to the process whereby knowledge relating to the transformation of inputs into outputs is acquired by entities within a country (for example, firms, research institutes, etc.) from sources outside that country. In examining the transfer of technology several points emerge.

The Creation of Knowledge
Knowledge is generally the result of the expenditure of human effort and material resources. This is so even when knowledge is a by-product, an unintended consequence of effort and resources expended for other purposes, as in the case of 'learning-by-doing' discussed in more detail in the later section on the sources of technical change. Since human effort and material resources can be put to uses other than the creation of knowledge, it is worth enquiring further into the factors determining the allocation of resources for the purposes of knowledge creation.

In a seminal paper, Arrow (1962a) has pointed out that difficult problems arise in capitalist societies in connection with the creation of knowledge. From society's point of view 'highly risky business activities, including invention ... should be undertaken if the expected return exceeds the market rate of return' (p. 168). However, 'any unwillingness and inability to bear risks will give rise to a non-optimal allocation of resources, in that there will be discrimination against risky enterprises as compared with the optimum' (p. 167).

With regard to willingness to invest resources for the purposes of creating knowledge two factors should be distinguished, both of which arise from the existence of uncertainty. (While a probability distribution can be derived in the case of risk as, for example, in insurance, this is not so in situations of uncertainty where, by definition, the future may be different from the past.) The first is that the outcome of attempts to create new knowledge is inherently uncertain. Certainty requires complete knowledge, which in turn precludes the possibility of creating new knowledge. Accordingly, efforts to create knowledge may or may not be successful. The second factor is that once knowledge has been created, it may be difficult to prevent its spread to other interested parties whose use of that knowledge may affect the returns derived by the original creator of the knowledge. This is the appropriability problem. Thus uncertainty is an important factor both before and after the creation of knowledge.

In view of this uncertainty, in capitalistic societies (to the extent that they revolve around private assessments of investment profitability) there may well be a reluctance that is undesirable from society's point of view to invest in the creation of knowledge. While in principle it is possible to shift the uncertainty from the inventor/innovator to those who provide the finance for the project (a point made by Schumpeter), in practice this possibility is limited by what Arrow refers to as the problem of 'moral hazard'; that is, although the uncertainty can be reduced, so too will be the return to the inventor/innovator and this raises the problem of incentive. For these reasons Arrow concludes that one would expect an underinvestment in knowledge-creating activities in a market economy.

The discussion so far, however, has implicitly assumed 'discrete jumps' in knowledge where the attendant uncertainties tend to be relatively great. This situation must be distinguished from incremental additions to knowledge, where the resources invested in knowledge-creation and the uncertainty are both smaller. Here the dilemmas noted by Arrow will not operate to the same extent. In many circumstances, however, studies suggest that the cumulative significance of such incremental changes may over time out-weigh that of radical change. In this connection see, for example, Usher (1954), Gilfillan (1953), Enos (1962) and Hollander (1965) for developed countries, and Katz (various), Dahlman and Fonseca (1978), Maxwell (1977, 1982), Lall (1982a) and Teitel (1984) for Third World countries. Accordingly, it is necessary to distinguish the magnitude of the change in knowledge that the investment is intended to bring about, and it is important not to underestimate the cumulative significance of more minor changes. These important points will re-emerge repeatedly in our subsequent discussions of technical change in Third World countries.

The Distribution of Knowledge
Since the acquisition of knowledge is costly in terms of human effort and material resources, and since these resources are (a) limited and (b) unevenly spread among entities acquiring knowledge, so knowledge will similarly be unevenly distributed. A further point is that the creation and acquisition of knowledge takes time. This is an additional factor making for an uneven distribution of knowledge at any point in time.

The uneven distribution of knowledge can present serious difficulties for the buyer of knowledge. Arrow (1962a) has pointed to 'a fundamental paradox in the determination of demand for information' (p. 171) arising from the fact that the purchaser is forced to make a bid for the information before being able to assess its value completely. In order to make a complete assessment the purchaser would have to possess the information before buying it, thus in effect acquiring it without cost. However, while this might pertain where there is only a small overlap between the information sets of the seller and buyer, in many other cases the buyer, while not possessing the same information as the seller, will nevertheless have 'some idea' of the likely benefits of the information. In other words, while the uneven distribution of knowledge will always imply a degree of uncertainty from the buyer's point of view, the degree itself, is variable.

It should be noted that these problems arising from the uneven distribution of knowledge will exist even where knowledge is non-proprietary. Imitation provides an example, although here the difficulty will arise, not in assessing the benefits of the knowledge, but in estimating the costs of acquiring that knowledge. The imitator initially possesses less information than the original producer and the costs of obtaining the knowledge necessary to imitate successfully will therefore be to some extent uncertain. Where the knowledge is proprietary, the problem is exacerbated because legal impediments are added to the factors inhibiting the flow of information.

The Price of Knowledge
What determines the price of knowledge? On both the supply and demand sides a number of factors must be taken into account. In the case of supply it must be recognised that knowledge has some of the attributes of 'public goods' in that the sale of knowledge does not reduce the magnitude of it available to the seller. Furthermore, the marginal cost of transmitting a given body of knowledge is frequently very low. However, the owner of knowledge is to some extent a monopolist and will usually be seeking to sell the knowledge at the highest possible price.

On the demand side, as we have seen, the buyer will be hindered by a greater or lesser degree of uncertainty in purchasing knowledge. Under these circumstances the price of knowledge will be indeterminate, ranging between a minimum level determined by the costs of producing that knowledge to a maximum amount determined by the buyer's estimate of the cost of the next best alternative (including going without the knowledge).

In view of the indeterminancy of the price of knowledge a good deal will depend on the relative bargaining strengths of the seller and buyer which, in turn, will depend on their respective resources, existing knowledge, and other alternatives. In the Third World context a good deal of attention has been paid to the ways in which Third World countries may reduce the price of the knowledge they purchase (see, for example, the work of Vaitsos (1974)).

Modes of Transfer of Knowledge

The diagram below presents a categorisation of some modes of transfer of knowledge.

	Active Role for Foreigners	Passive Role for Foreigners
Formal (market-mediated)	Direct foreign invest-ment, Joint venture, Turnkey project, Management con-tract, Licensing	Machinery purchase
Informal (non-market-mediated)	Learning-by-export-ing	Imitation Trade journals, etc. Scientific exchange

This categorisation is constructed on the basis of two primary distinctions. The first, introduced by Dahlman and Westphal (1982) relates to the extent to which foreigners are active or passive in the transfer. The second relates to whether the transfer is formal (that is, market-mediated) or informal (that is, non-market-mediated). These distinctions allow us to identify different modes of knowledge transfer.

Most attention has been devoted to the examination of those modes included in the north-west rectangle. These include direct foreign investment, joint ventures, management contracts, turnkey projects, and licensing and other technology agreements. In all these cases foreigners play an active role in the transfer, influencing the quantity and quality of knowledge transferred, the circumstances under which it is transferred, including factors such as the restrictions that will be imposed on the use of the knowledge, and the price of the knowledge. The transfer itself is market-mediated.

Machinery purchase serves as the major example of transfer

in the north-east rectangle. Here too the transfer is market-mediated, but foreigners play a relatively passive role and usually do not exercise much control over the way in which the knowledge, embodied in the machinery, is used by the buyer. Machinery purchase has been an important source of knowledge in the Third World.

In the case of the major transfer in the south-west rectangle, learning-by-exporting, foreigners play an active role. In this case, however, the foreigners transfer knowledge to exporting firms regarding the shortcomings of their products and the improvements that may be made. The most intensively studied case is South Korea (see Westphal, Rhee and Pursell, 1984; Dahlman and Westphal, 1982) where it has been concluded that an important source of knowledge for firms in the export sector has been provided by users and sellers in export markets. Here foreigners play an active role in that the transfer of knowledge is dependent on their decisions. However, the transfer is non-market mediated in the sense that the knowledge is seldom sold at a price. None the less, Westphal and his collaborators show that this mode of knowledge transfer, although not yet very well studied, has been extremely important as a source of product, and in some cases process, improvement.

In the south-west rectangle are modes of knowledge transfer which are usually non-market-mediated and in which foreigners play a relatively passive role. Once again, however, these have constituted important means whereby knowledge has been transferred to Third World countries. In the three examples given, imitation, scientific exchange and trade journals, while foreigners do not decide to transfer knowledge, and therefore in this sense are passive, their knowledge is nevertheless transferred to Third World users. In these cases it is the latter who actively facilitate the transfer. (Examples studied include steel production in Brazil (Dahlman and Fonseca, 1978) and CNC machine tools in Taiwan (Fransman, forthcoming).)

While the best studied have been formal transfers where foreigners play an active role, the other transfers of knowledge which are non-market-mediated and in which foreigners play a more passive role are also important under particular circumstances and require further attention. In general they refer to instances involving incremental improvements in knowledge but over time their cumulative effects might be extremely important.

(a) *Direct costs of knowledge transfer:* A good deal of attention has been paid in the literature on technology in the Third World to the direct costs of formal technology transfer where foreigners play an active role. (See, for example, the reviews referred to at the beginning of this section.) Direct costs are either overt or hidden. Overt costs appear in the contracted price (for example, the price of the turnkey project) while the hidden costs are implicit. The latter include restrictive clauses and transfer pricing. Both overt and hidden costs are direct in that they refer to the cost of purchasing the knowledge itself. Indirect costs will be considered below, the most important of which is the influence of the imported knowledge on local knowledge-creating capabilities.

The literature on formal technology transfers which involve an active role for foreigners has considered the transfer from the point of view of both the seller and buyer. The seller, attempting to get the highest price for the knowledge being sold, will try as far as possible to monopolise that knowledge. By 'packaging' the knowledge, that is, by combining all the elements of the transfer (such as the engineering work, supply of machinery and equipment, and training) into one 'package', the seller may be able to obtain a higher price (both overt and hidden) than if the elements were sold separately. In general, the greater the seller's monopoly over the knowledge, and the greater the buyer's need for that knowledge (and the less feasible the buyer's alternatives), the greater will be the seller's options. Sellers in a very strong position may only be willing to transfer the knowledge where they retain maximum control over its use such as in the case of wholly-owned subsidiaries. The Japanese experience has shown dramatically that in the case of other formal modes of transfer, such as the sale of turnkey projects or licensing, the seller's degree of control may, over time, be whittled away. Conversely, the buyer may be attempting[3] to reduce the seller's monopoly power through means such as negotiating with several sellers simultaneously and trying to 'unpackage' the technology. The relative bargaining strengths of buyer and seller will determine the ultimate deal that is struck.

Far less attention, however, has been paid to the costs and benefits of informal transfers of knowledge where foreigners play a relatively passive role. Dahlman and Westphal (1982), for example, suggest that the knowledge that is acquired indirectly through the feedback that exporters receive is virtually costless while it provides important benefits. However, even here the recipient firm will have to devote resources to transforming the feedback flow of information into improved products and processes. Similarly, in the case of imitation, the use of foreign trade journals, and scientific exchanges, the allocation of local resources will be necessary in the first instance to search for the appropriate foreign knowledge, and secondly, to use it effectively.

(b) *Quality of the knowledge transferred:* Account must also be taken of the quality of the knowledge transferred. In the case of direct foreign investment, for example, Lall (1984) has shown that sophisticated processes and products may be transferred without the ability to design and change the products or substantially modify the processes. The latter capabilities are frequently centralised in developed countries. In such cases, Lall suggests, know-how rather than know-why is being transferred. However, it is not at all obvious that in all circumstances know-why is more desirable than know-how. To begin with, know-why may be more costly to obtain, and secondly, for some purposes it may not be necessary. For example, to use a machine will require less knowledge than to design a machine but in some circumstances efficient use of machinery is sufficient. Nevertheless, in order to take account of both costs and benefits it is necessary to assess the quality of the knowledge that is being transferred

Local Knowledge-Creating Capabilities
While the bulk of the literature on the transfer of technology

until the late 1970s tended to concentrate on the overt and hidden direct costs, attention since has increasingly focused on the importance of local knowledge-creating capabilities. For reasons that will be elaborated upon later, it came to be understood that local 'knowledge' plays an important role in any transfer of foreign knowledge.[4] An important insight in this context came from Nelson (1978) who stressed the 'implicitness' and 'tacitness' inherent in any technology transfer. Nelson pointed out that technological knowledge, as a result of its complexity, cannot be transferred in its entirety. The result is that the purchaser of technology *always* receives a less complete information set than possessed by the seller, despite the transfer of blueprints, instructions, etc. Furthermore, the context within which the technology will be used will always differ, to a greater or lesser extent, between firms. Accordingly, *any* technology transfer, including an international transfer of technology, requires a degree of technological capability on the part of the receiving firm. While the technological capability required will depend on the complexity of the transferred technology, in general the greater the extent of this capability, the more likely is a successful transfer.

However, while local technological knowledge may always be required in order to facilitate an effective use of foreign knowledge, account must be taken of the possible existence of complementarities and substitutabilities between foreign and local technological knowledge. In the case of complementarity, the large number of studies done under the direction of Katz (various) in Latin America have shown that foreign knowledge may stimulate the development of local knowledge-creating capabilities. However, there is also the possibility that these local capabilities may be undermined by the use of foreign knowledge, or at least not encouraged to the extent that they might be. It is for this reason that both Katz and Lall, drawing on the Latin American and Indian cases, have concluded that in some situations the protection of local knowledge-creating capabilities may be justified. Furthermore, Cooper (1980) has suggested that the social benefits of local knowledge creation may outweigh the private benefits, with the result that less knowledge is created locally than is desirable. He takes as an example engineering subcontracting where contracts are given to foreign firms as a result of their 'reputation' rather than to local firms with less experience. From the point of view of local knowledge-creating capabilities, the difference in quality, etc. between the foreign and local engineering subcontractors may be more than outweighed by the social benefits of the additional capabilities that are generated. Yet in the absence of state intervention, foreign engineering subcontractors may be preferred.

While the effect on local knowledge-creating capabilities must always be assessed in any examination of the costs and benefits of alternative modes of knowledge transfer, it must be remembered that technological knowledge is usually not an end in itself. 'More' knowledge is not always to be preferred to 'less' knowledge. Some knowledge may not be necessary for the attainment of the objectives that have been chosen. Accordingly, account must also be taken of the ultimate objectives in assessing local knowledge-creating capabilities.

CHOICE OF TECHNIQUE AND APPROPRIATE TECHNOLOGY

Analyses of choice of technique and of appropriate technology are conceptually related. At first glance the issues are relatively straightforward. First, it is necessary to establish the choice set by identifying all those techniques that are technically efficient. A technique is technically inefficient relative to other techniques if it requires more of at least one input while using no less of all the other inputs. An efficient technique in one which is not inefficient. Second, the appropriate technique is that within the choice set which yields the greatest social benefit to cost ratio.[5]

The first-glance simplicity is, however, deceptive for reasons which include the following. First, as Sen (1980) points out, 'technical efficiency cannot be taken to be either necessary or sufficient for social optimality, given the special characteristics of labour' (p. 124). The problem here is that labour is not only a factor of production; it is also a goal of production. To illustrate this Sen takes the example of technique A which is assumed to require less labour than technique B. However, the workers concerned prefer to work longer hours under B: '"It is more interesting work" or "one is ordered around less" or "I hate those production belts of A"', etc. Sen points out:

While technique A may be efficient, which B is not, B could still be taken to be superior from the social point of view. This will be the case if the value put on the labourers' excess suffering from working fewer hours under A rather than more hours under B is greater than the saving, if any, of other resources under A. Inefficiency is no longer a sufficient ground for rejection. The fact that one of the resources is labour has changed all that. (p. 123)

Nevertheless, Sen does argue that inefficiency provides a *prima facie* case against a technique and good reasons would have to be given if a technically inefficient technique is to be chosen.

Second, Sen (1980) also points out that the evaluation of social benefits can prove to be an extremely complicated, if not impossible, task. For present purposes a good example of this is the effect of choosing a particular technique on learning and the creation of skills. A technique that is technically inefficient in the short run may turn out to be efficient over time as a result of such learning and skill effects. However, including these effects in the calculation is inherently difficult. 'If learning could be taken to be an "output" in the usual sense, then it could become a part of the efficiency calculation itself. But it is not easy to identify learning as an output, and it is not really surprising that the usual economic calculations of inputs and outputs tend to leave it out' (p.125). Nevertheless, Sen warns, 'The Scylla of assuming without demonstration that a justification in terms of learning does exist is no less to be avoided than the Charybdis of taking it implicitly for granted that such a demonstration could not really exist' (pp. 125–6). The correct evaluation of dynamic effects such as these clearly raises important analytical and measurement problems.

Thirdly, while it is usual to insist on the use of shadow prices in the evaluation of social costs and benefits in Third World countries, this in turn can present further difficulties. To begin with:

shadow prices themselves introduce problems of their own. In some cases, for example, where there are strong increasing returns, shadow prices simply may not exist. Furthermore, even when they do exist in principle, they are typically based on educated guesses; the increased sophistication of shadow price estimation methods should not blind their users to that fact (Sen, 1980: 126–7)

Furthermore, in some situations social cost-benefit analysis will not be the only appropriate analytical tool. For example, in the case of bargaining with the technology supplier it will be important to know, not only about the social costs and benefits from the point of view of the purchaser, but also about the seller's costs and benefits.

Only in a situation of one party is it sufficient to use the standard techniques of cost benefit analysis, that is, examining net benefits for oneself only. Whenever there are several parties with part coincidence, part conflict, of interests, there is scope for 'adversary analysis'. There is then a need to play the dialectical role of placing oneself in the position of one's adversary and seeing what things look like from that end of the 'bargaining problem'. (ibid., 136–7)

An ambitious but potentially promising attempt to move in the direction suggested by Sen is Enos's (1984) application of the game-theoretic approach to the problem of choice of technique in Third World countries.

A fourth complication arises from a definition of technology and technique which includes products as well as inputs required in the production of a given output. Accordingly, a consideration of choice of technique and appropriateness of technology must also involve an examination of products. This question has been most closely examined by Stewart and also by James. In Stewart and James (1982) the Lancaster framework is used in order to examine products in terms of their characteristics and in this way to examine the welfare effects of the introduction of new products.

Fifth, the conventional discussion of choice of technique, as

Nelson (1978) points out, implicitly makes unrealistic and misleading assumptions regarding the state of knowledge:

There doesn't exist a well-defined set of 'technological options' out there that a firm can scan and assess easily and reliably. This is not to deny that there [is] a wide range of choice, and that finding out about the options and thinking about the choices isn't important. However, it is likely to be a far more difficult matter than generally assumed for a firm to be able to judge how a particular technique employed by another firm would operate for it. Its own version of the technique invariably would involve a variety of idiosyncracies, some intended and some not. Invariably, there would be teething problems, and the need to learn-by-doing, and perhaps by researching. (p. 18)

This perspective suggests that one important aspect of the 'selection environment' is the knowledge possessed by the selector and the costs of alternative ways of obtaining knowledge. It suggests, furthermore, that technological capabilities will play an important role in facilitating adequate choice of technique and in making the technique work in a satisfactory manner, once chosen.

Finally, the importance of indigenous technological capabilities also emerges from the realisation that the choice set is itself changing over time. As Bhalla (1981) puts it: 'Most empirical case studies are focused on the question of choosing from a set of alternatives at a given point in time, thus largely neglecting the process whereby new technology is developed, applied and diffused' (p. 377). Thus a further dimension that must of necessity be taken into account in evaluating appropriateness and choice of technique relates to likely future technological developments. It is hardly necessary to point to the additional complications that this presents.

The empirical issue of the substitutability of different inputs (usually capital and labour) is of particular concern to economists of a neoclassical persuasion who stress the importance of factor substitution in response to changing relative factor prices. One method which has been used in the attempt to measure factor substitutability is the estimation of the elasticity of substitution of labour for capital using a constant elasticity of substitution (CES) production function.

However, the results of this line of research have been less than encouraging. In a review of the empirical evidence Gaude (1981) asks 'whether the elasticity of substitution can in any way be measured, so as to constitute an adequate indicator of actual economic behaviour'. His conclusion is that 'the difficulties of comparison ... render estimates of the elasticity of substitution a doubtful indicator on which to base economic policy formulation' (p. 63).

Similarly, White (1978) concludes that the 'econometric evidence probably does give some support for the proposition that efficient labour-intensive alternatives for manufacturing exist. But this is probably more an act of faith than a hard conclusion from incontrovertible evidence'. However, other investigations have provided more evidence of substitutability and the viability of labour-intensive techniques. These include studies based on engineering production functions and process analysis. In reviewing these White concludes that: 'In all, the engineering and process-analysis studies do provide powerful demonstrations of the feasibility of labour-intensive methods and are probably more convincing than the econometric studies'. The general conclusion that emerges from these and other case studies is that there is scope for choosing more labour-intensive techniques, although the range of choice varies between industries. Thus Dahlman and Westphal (1982) conclude: 'It is now well established that there is scope for choosing between techniques with differing levels of labour intensity and productivity, but that the scope for choice is by no means uniform' (pp. 109–10). Similarly, Forsyth, McBain and Solomon (1982) find evidence for substantial factor substitution in Third World countries. They develop an 'Index of Technical Rigidity' on the basis of eight 'fundamental physical barriers to the substitution of labour for capital'. They conclude that scale is also important in determining factor use.

However, not all writers have drawn the same inferences from these conclusions. Some, like Stewart, have argued that despite the substitutability, techniques and products developed in the highly industrialised countries tend very often to be inappropriate in terms of Third World resources and needs. In direct contrast Little (1982) concludes that the recent stress on the inappropriateness of existing technology has been overdone. The earlier version – that one of the great advantages of backwardness is that more modern techniques can be acquired from abroad far more cheaply than they can be developed and invented, is still valid ... Korea, Taiwan and Hong Kong have shown that a sufficiently labour-intensive development was possible without any need to develop *new* labour-intensive methods. (p.181)

3 Technical Change in the Third World

DEFINING TECHNICAL CHANGE

In this chapter technology refers to those activities involved in the transforming of inputs into outputs. Hence technical change refers to changes in these activities. This definition is to be contrasted with the more conventional one whereby 'technology' refers to the totality of alternative combinations of inputs (or 'techniques') required to produce a given output. The present definition focuses attention on the transformation process itself, on what goes on inside the 'black box' into which inputs go, and out of which outputs come. Further discussion of the transformation process, however, is reserved for section IV dealing with the sources of technical change.

FORMS OF TECHNICAL CHANGE IN THE THIRD WORLD

The following forms of technological change occur in the Third World:

(1) The Search for New Products and Processes
It has been emphasised in the literature that search activity, while costly, requires the firm to possess the necessary technological capabilities. A certain amount of knowledge is

necessary for the firm to gain additional knowledge through its search processes. Search may include relatively 'passive' activities such as the scanning of trade journals as well as more 'active' testing of alternative processes and products. (The search metaphor, as opposed to the notion of choice of technique, is itself of interest since it implies to a greater extent the existence of uncertainty and the possibility of failure.)

(2) The Adaptation of Products and Processes to Local Conditions

As mentioned earlier, technology is *always* to some extent implicit and location-specific. Accordingly, *any* transfer of technology will require a degree of adaptation. However, in the literature a number of conditions have been singled out as being particularly important in the Third World context. These include the size and characteristics of local markets, the degree of competition in protected markets, the availability of different kinds of skilled labour, and the supply and quality of local resources. (See, for example, the various writings of Katz and Teitel for the Latin American case, and Lall for India.) These writers have stressed that adaptation is not always socially progressive as in the case, for example, where adjustments are required by 'irrational' government policy.

(3) Improving Products and Processes

Here activities go beyond adapting the production and sale of products and processes to local conditions and involve their improvement in various ways.[6] These improvements may be incremental and minor, or they may be major, involving discrete jumps at a point in time. However, the cumulative significance of incremental improvements over time may be great. We shall see later that such improvements, taking place within Third World conditions, have resulted in 'technological trajectories' different from those in the highly industrialised countries. In turn these have resulted in exports of technology in various forms from the more industrialised Third World countries.

(4) Developing 'New' Products and Processes

Here it is necessary to distinguish processes and products that are 'new' from the point of view of the firm, the industry, the country, and the world. Applying our earlier definitions at the level of the firm, we would regard the production of products or processes that are new to the firm as involving technical change. In general Third World countries will very rarely produce products and processes that are in a fundamental sense new to the world.

(5) Basic Research

While there is relatively little basic research in Third World countries, these activities do exist. This raises the question of how much basic research is justifiable and desirable at any time in any particular country. A further problem which has been discussed in the literature is the question of the relationship between scientific and technical institutions and production and exchange activities in the economy. (See, for example, Cooper, 1973a and b; Crane, 1977; Clark and Parthasarathi, 1982). These issues will be pursued later.

Several points need to be made about the above categorisation of technological activities in the Third World. To begin with it should be realised that the 'stock' of capabilities required for these activities does not necessarily increase as we move from (1) to (5). For example, it may be a far more complex matter, requiring greater technological capabilities, to search for an appropriate petrochemical plant, than to design a new, but relatively simple, machine. Nevertheless, and despite this last example, there will often be a qualitative distinction between the first three forms of technological change and the last two. To some extent the difference is captured by the distinction, introduced in this context by Lall, between knowing how something works, and knowing why it works in the way it does. The implication is that in moving from the former to the latter there is a qualitative increase in the 'depth of knowledge' required (measured, perhaps, by the cost of acquiring the knowledge).

To illustrate this point further, and make finer discriminations, there is a qualitative distinction between: (a) searching for and using a machine; (b) repairing a machine; (c) imitating and adapting a machine for local production and sale; (d) improving the machine; (e) designing and developing a new machine; and (f) basic research on the underlying principles that can be applied in the creation of machinery. In general, there will be an increase in the required depth of knowledge as we move up these activities.

A further implication raises the important question of the 'depth' of knowledge required by a country's various activities at any particular stage of its industrialisation. The importance of this question is grasped once the link is made between depth and the cost of acquiring technological knowledge. But how do we decide on the depth that is appropriate in any particular case? This question is difficult to answer. However, a number of relevant points have emerged in the literature. One of these is that relatively deep levels of technological knowledge are not necessary in the earlier stages of industrialisation. Thus Dahlman and Westphal (1982) argue that 'As Korean experience demonstrates, ... high indigenous levels of all types of technological mastery are not necessary for the initial stages of industrial development; in the Korean case, a mastery which has been mainly confined to production engineering has been sufficient' (p. 133). Another point, made by Lall (1984a) is that deeper forms of technological knowledge are not necessarily more socially beneficial than those that are 'shallow'. Ranis (1977, 1984), Dore (1984) and others have noted that the gradual progression from 'lower' to 'deeper' forms of technological knowledge has played a central role in Japanese industrialisation. The same point is related to South Korea in Kim (1980). We shall return to this question later in connection with the international diffusion of technology and the 'catch-up' process, and the question of infant industries.

There is widespread agreement in the literature that Third World technological activity is on the whole confined to (1) to (3) above. Fairly typical is Katz's (1984) observation that:

specialised technical departments of medium size and large firms ... generate incremental units of technical knowledge in the areas of product design, process engineering and production planning and organization. They adapt foreign technology to the local environment and gradually build up a stock of proprietary technology and know-how highly specific to the firm. It is here where domestic technological capabilities actually appear and develop (pp. 2, 3)

As Lall (1982a) points out, these activities will usually be well within the international technology frontier.

Third World technological activity, accordingly, tends to be almost exclusively of the incremental kind rather than of the Schumpeterian frontier-moving type. To the extent that the latter occurs within the Third World, it is the result of technology generated abroad rather than indigenous efforts. However, it is important not to underestimate the cumulative significance of incremental technological change. The point is not a new one, though social scientists of technology have often been blinded by the dazzling brilliance of major innovations. It goes back at least to the work of Usher on mechanical inventions and Gilfillan on innovations relating to the ship in 1929 (1954) and 1935 (1935), respectively. More recently, the same point has been made by Hollander (1965) in his discussion of DuPont's rayon plants and Enos's (1962) study of petroleum refining. Accordingly, it would be wrong to underestimate the significance of the forms of technological change occurring within Third World countries.

Several authors have attempted to identify stages in the development of technological capabilities in Third World countries (see, *inter alia*, Cortez, 1978; Lall, 1980a; Katz, 1984a, 1984b; Kit, 1980; Teitel, 1981, 1984). While the reader may refer to these sources for details of the stages identified, several more general points will be made here. The first is that, as discussed above, the task of identifying stages of progression is inherently difficult as a result of the problem of generalising about degrees of complexity regarding techno-logical capabilities. For example, the learning-by-doing process in the production of jet-engines may require more complex (and costly) technological capabilities than the design of conventional machine-tools. Second, there is always a danger with 'stage theories' than an overly mechanistic account is given of the transition from one stage to the next. A closer examination often shows that the order implied by the stage description is not always adhered to. Lastly, and most significantly, stage 'theories' often lack a convincing *explanation* of the causal mechanism whereby one stage progresses into another. These points have been very well understood, and made explicit by authors who, despite the difficulties, have nevertheless found it helpful to think in terms of a technological progression over time.

MEASURING TECHNOLOGICAL CHANGE

Technical change, defined in this Part as changes in the way in which inputs are transformed into outputs, including the production of improved outputs, is inherently difficult to measure. The principal reason is that the transformation process involved in production is extremely complex with the result that it is difficult to establish a measure, or measures, of this process. Accordingly, technical change has usually been measured *indirectly*, rather than attempting to find a measure of the transformation process itself. For convenience it will be useful to divide these measures into three categories: first, output measures of technical change; second, measures of technical change inputs; third, measures that relate output to inputs.

The first, and most important, thing to note about these measures is that since the technical change process itself is not being measured, we are unable from the measures to throw light on the *causes* of such change. This emerges in a discussion of a measure in the third category, namely, total factor productivity. A change in total factor productivity may be the result of technical change within the country, sector or firm, or it may be the result of external factors such as the purchase of more efficient inputs (like new machinery) which do not require much internal technical change. Furthermore, if the former is the case, the change in total factor productivity measured may be the result of a large number of possible causal circumstances. Accordingly, in order to provide an understanding of the causes of technical change it is necessary to go one step further and examine the relationship between such circumstances and the measure of technical change that has been chosen. An example of such a study is Dahlman (1981) which examines the relationship between various capacity-stretching innovations and total factor productivity change. Given the diversity of firms, studies like these will often be of the micro case-study type.

Quite apart from the obvious, though often forgotten observation that the measures of technical change usually used do not illuminate the causes of technical change, the measures themselves have serious shortcomings. In the case of output measures, for example, there is widespread agreement that there is no entirely satisfactory measure. One such measure which has been frequently used in the context of developed countries is patent data. However, as is well known,[7] patents suffer a number of important drawbacks if used as an indicator of technical change. For example, patents are often not used; it is extremely difficult, if not impossible, to weight patents in order to aggregate them; for a large number of reasons innovations are often not patented; and, perhaps most important for the Third World context, patents do not capture the incremental forms of technical change that will often be of central significance. Another possible output measure of technical change is output itself which is used, of course, in measures of productivity. However, a major problem here is the difficulty of measuring quality improvements, with the result, as Rosenberg (1982) notes, that improvements in product quality are often ignored. Case studies, dealing in greater detail with specific products, may be more amenable to a quantification of product change. A further output measure of technical change that has been used in some of the literature on the Third World involves the selection of a specific category of output, namely, exports (and at times a sub-set of this category, namely technology exports). The main reason behind the choice of this measure is that, since trade restrictions are so important in Third World countries, it is only exports that meet international efficiency criteria.

Exports can accordingly be used as an indication of the technical capability of firms. However, as we shall see in a later discussion of technology exports, exports may be the result either of factor cost differences or of successful technical change. To the extent that the former is the case, exports will be an inadequate indicator of technical change. Furthermore, change in exports may be the result of changes in international or national circumstances rather than technical change as such. Accordingly it will be necessary to control for these other influences on exports.

Input measures of technical change also face severe limitations. A general difficulty is that if they are used alone, rather than in conjunction with another measure such as output in the case of a measure of productivity, they may be misleading since they bear no necessary relationship to output. For example, measures such as total spending on R & D, science and technology personnel (perhaps weighted to take account of training and experience), etc. may fail to provide an indication of technical change since it is the *output* of such resources that is significant. Furthermore, as Kamien and Schwartz (1982) point out:

A particular shortcoming is that research and development spending is treated as a flow cost rather than as an investment. This method ignores the accumulation of knowledge and know-how through time that in fact constitutes an asset. Thus a potentially important input into the innovation process, accumulated knowledge, is left out when current expenditures alone measure innovative input. (p. 51)

As with the firm's capital stock in general, there are inherent difficulties in calculating the present discounted value of this particular asset. In addition, measures such as R & D expenditure and science and technology personnel fail to capture other inputs into the technical change process emanating from elsewhere in the firm such as production engineers, worker suggestions, etc.

In view of difficulties such as these it will usually be necessary to combine a number of measures of technical change. At the beginning of this section we raised the question of the relationship between the causes and the measurement of technical change. In the following section we shall examine further some of the sources of technical change.

4 Sources of Technical Change

'Firms' purchase inputs and transform them into outputs. In section 3 we defined technical *change* as changes in the way in which inputs are transformed into outputs. The starting point in the analysis of technical change is an examination of the 'firm'.

THE FIRM

In approaching the firm it is heuristically useful to begin with the neoclassical perspective since it has been dominant in economics. As Nelson (1981) points out,[8] in the neoclassical approach,

Firms are the key productive actors, transforming inputs into outputs according to a production function. The production function, which defines the maximum output achievable with any given quantity of inputs, is determined by the state of technological knowledge. Technological knowledge is assumed to be public or at least this is implicit in models based on an industry or an economy-wide production function. Firms choose a point on their production function to maximise profits, given product demand and factor supply conditions ... Over time, output grows as inputs increase and firms move along their production functions, and as technology advances. (p. 1031)

There are a number of problems with this approach which hinder an understanding of the process of technical change. Some of the major problems will be discussed briefly here.

The first problem is that the neoclassical view implicitly assumes a single decision-making centre within the firm. This centre makes profit-maximising decisions on the basis of the given technology and the array of factor and product prices and these decisions are automatically, and successfully, implemented within the firm. This assumption, however, obscures a number of processes within firms that have a central bearing on technical change. Changes in the way inputs are transformed into outputs are not the result of the 'decisions' made by 'management', but the outcome of an interactive process involving *all* the firm's employees, including its management. Rather than a homogeneous entity, firms are divided into constituent components that are hierarchically structured. The further up the hierarchy, the greater the degree of 'autonomy' in decision-making. However, in examining the functioning of the hierarchy two points should be noted. The first is that most, if not all, decisions taken at the top of the hierarchy will be the result of a process of negotiation between individuals and groups that exercise power within the organisation. For example, a decision to invest in new equipment may be the result of prior negotiation between the finance, production and marketing departments. It is not at all clear that the perspectives and degrees of influence of the heads of the sub-hierarchies in these departments will be the same. The 'decision' that is ultimately taken by the 'firm' will be the result of the negotiations and power of these sub-hierarchies. Second, in examining the functioning of the hierarchy it is necessary to distinguish between 'decisions' made at the top of the hierarchy and the implementation of those decisions. Clearly the ultimate effect of the decisions will be influenced by the degree of success with which they are implemented. In this connection Nelson (1981) has argued that the firm is in fact 'a social system which may be resistant or unresponsive to management commands'. He suggests that 'in general, the employees of firms do not automatically share the same objectives as managers. So there is a requirement for motivation and monitoring' (pp. 1037–8). Accordingly, in order to understand the changes that occur within the firm in the transforming of inputs into outputs, it is necessary to understand the organisational complexities of the firm. Such an understanding will take us at least part of the way towards an explanation of inter-firm and inter-country differences in the process of technical change.[9]

The importance of this abstract discussion emerges when more concrete questions are posed. Why, for example, have many large Japanese firms performed better, in terms of the price and quality of their output, than many of their Western rivals? In the vast literature that has emerged on this question one consistent theme has focused on the social relations existing within Japanese firms.[10] In view of the cumulative significance of incremental technical change referred to above, it is increasingly being realised that ultimate improvements in product quality and price result not only from the firm's R & D efforts but also from the more obscure activities of other personnel such as production engineers and workers, as the frequent success of quality circles has shown. For these reasons it is misleading to conceptualise the firm in terms of a single decision-making centre which maximises profits given the existing state of technical knowledge and the array of factor and product prices. Such a view is incapable of answering questions such as the one we have posed about Japanese economic performance.

In the Third World context the view of the firm as a social system raises numerous questions that have not begun to be asked. By and large the question of technical change has been posed in terms of differences in the firm's external environments in different Third World countries. These differences include the degree of liberalisation in international trade flows, other government incentives and disincentives, etc. On the basis of an examination of these environmental differences and an evaluation of economic performance, attempts have been made to assess the costs and benefits of alternative environmental variables. However, no account has been taken of possible inter-firm and inter-country differences in social organisation. The Japanese example suggests that this might be a serious oversight.

A second problem with the conventional neoclassical approach arises from the assumption that the 'state of technical knowledge' is 'given' to the firm. This assumption ignores the fact that a good deal of technical knowledge is firm-specific rather than being evenly distributed amongst firms.[11] The acquisition of additional technical knowledge, even if it exists elsewhere, will therefore be costly, to a greater or lesser extent, in terms of the expenditure of firm resources. Furthermore, the acquiring of new knowledge is always an uncertain process. In view of the uncertainty there will frequently be a degree of doubt regarding desirable paths of future development for the firm. This doubt will form a potential basis for differences between the different sub-hierarchies in the firm. By assuming that technology is 'given' to all firms, the neoclassical approach shifts attention away from the processes referred to here which have a central bearing on technical change and therefore on the performance of firms, industries and countries.

CONTINUITY AND CHANGE

In the stationary state, where the world of tomorrow will be in all essential respects identical with that of today, there is by definition perfect certainty and no technical change. Over time firms and consumers will adapt to their changeless environment eventually reaching their preferred positions. From this point on the transformation of inputs into outputs and consumption will involve repetition, continuity rather than change. Since all firms and consumers will be in their desired positions and since the changeless world will ensure that these desires are not frustrated, general equilibrium will exist.

While economists throughout the ages have found it heuristically useful to examine various properties of the stationary state, this state of affairs stands in strong contrast to the real world. In the real world change is the rule rather than the exception. Limiting ourselves to production, to those activities involved in the transformation of inputs into outputs, it is worth asking why in the real world, firms change. In answering this question Schumpeter, in *Capitalism, Socialism and Democracy* (1966) points to pressures from other firms exerted through competition.

Competition
Schumpeter notes that:

> capitalist economy is not and cannot be stationary. Nor is it merely expanding in a steady manner. It is incessantly being revolutionized *from within* by new enterprise, i.e. by the intrusion of new commodities or new methods of production or new commercial opportunities into the industrial structure as it exists at any moment. Any existing structures and all the conditions of doing business are always in a process of change. Every situation is being upset before it has had time to work itself out . . .. Possibilities of gains to be reaped by producing new things or by producing old things more cheaply are constantly materializing and calling for new investments. These new products and new methods compete with the old products and old methods not on equal terms but at a decisive advantage that may mean death to the latter. This is how 'progress' comes about in capitalist society. In order to escape being undersold, *every* firm is in the end compelled to follow suit, to invest in its turn and, in order to be able to do so, to plow back part of its profits, i.e. to accumulate. Thus, everyone else accumulates. (1966: 31–2)[12]

Two related aspects of the process described by Schumpeter deserve to be underscored. The first is that in order to understand some aspects of the technical change process, it is necessary to examine the firm in relationship to the other firms producing for the same markets. Where purchasers can choose between the products of different firms, the activities of these firms will be intimately related to each other. *In this situation it is invalid to focus attention solely on the individual firm as the unit of analysis.*

The second aspect of the Schumpeterian process of economic change is that every firm is 'compelled' to change by the fact, or threat, of cheaper and/or 'better' products being made available by competing firms. Failure to change will result in reduced revenues, or revenues increasing at a slower rate than they might if change were undertaken. The compulsion or pressure which is in this way brought to bear on firms and which may result in firms undertaking technical change must be distinguished from the *incentives* that the firm may have to change. The reason for distinguishing between pressures and incentives is that, as Rosenberg (1976) has noted, there may be an asymmetry between them: 'It is possible ... that threats of deterioration or actual deterioration from some previous state are more powerful attention-focusing devices that are vague possibilities for improvement' (p. 124). We shall return later to a more detailed discussion of some of the incentives which have been identified as motivations for technical change.

In analysing the effect of the pressure that is brought to bear on firms through competition it is necessary to bear in mind that firms are complex social entities and that in this respect no two firms are identical. Greater variations may exist between firms in different countries as a result of the specific pattern of social relations pertaining in each country. One consequence is that there is no reason to expect that firms will react in the same way, or equally successfully, when similar pressure is exerted on them. When the firm's products lag behind the leaders in terms of price and/or quality, change will be obligatory (unless the firm is to become extinct or be subsidised) but the nature and success of the change will depend on a large number of firm-specific factors. Accordingly, a divergence between best and average practice will be the rule. Some firms of course may sink.

Economists in developed countries have paid a good deal of attention to the relationship between market structure (that is, degree of competition) and innovation—with the causation running in both directions. While very firm conclusions have not been reached, it is worth reporting the findings of a recent comprehensive survey of research on these countries: 'an industry with many moderate to large firms of relatively similar size and with a growing scientific base will tend to be the most technologically progressive. Neither the extremes of perfect competition nor perfect monopoly appear to be most conducive to technical advance (Kamien and Schwartz, 1982: 53).

In view of the conclusion about high degrees of competition, and in the light of the discussion above on the pressures that competition exerts on firms, it is of some interest to note that Japanese policy-makers have at times felt that 'excessive' competition can be harmful. Thus Peck and Tamura (1976) note that 'with the goals of avoiding excessive competition and realising economies of scale and at the same time establishing several competitors in each industry, the Ministry of International Trade and Industry (MITI), it is widely believed, showed more concern about the risks of too much rather than too little competition' (p. 558). Various industries were also given protection from foreign competition during the post-Second World War period.

In the Third World context the question of competition assumes a special significance. The reason is that most Third World countries have had, and continue to have, high effective rates of protection in various sectors of their economies. Coupled frequently with minimal exports of manufactured goods and low levels of domestic competition this has meant that competitive pressures for technical change have often been limited. In turn this has led to debates about the costs and benefits of increasing international competition, an issue that is pursued in a later section in this article dealing with infant industries.

However, there is a good deal of evidence to suggest that despite the relative absence of competitive pressures in places such as the Latin American countries and India, there is nevertheless much technical change. Katz (1984b) and Teitel (1984) for Latin America and Lall (1984b) for India have shown that in more protected environments with relatively limited domestic competition technical change is oriented largely to overcoming bottlenecks in supplies of intermediates and raw materials (in terms of both quantity and quality). Conversely, in much of the Third World literature, the hypothesis has been put forward that the greater the degree of competition in domestic and/or foreign markets, the greater the dominance of cost-cutting and quality-increasing innovations.

This discussion of technical change in the absence of

external competitive pressures raises the question of the effects of 'incentives' of various kinds and it is to this that we now turn.

Information Flows, Learning and Incentives

The activity of transforming inputs into outputs involves knowledge of how to do things, although not necessarily knowledge of why things work in the way they do. The activities of buying, producing and selling, in addition to the purchase, production and sale of actual goods and services, also provide sources of new information for firms. The purchase of improved components, or of labour with new skills, for example, will provide the firm with new information, and therefore new possibilities. Similarly, the activity of production will generate information flows which may form the basis for subsequent improvement. One specific example, discussed at length by Rosenberg (1976) is the emergence of bottlenecks within and between interdependent production processes which 'throw off signals' which point to the advantages that would be derived from solutions to the underlying constraints. These signals initiate what Rosenberg refers to as 'compulsive sequences' in technical change. The same point is made by Hughes (1984) in his historical study of electricity generation using the military concept of the 'reverse salient' which also signals priorities for attention.[13] The activities involved in selling will also generate flows of new information. Some of these flows will occur even in the absence of competitive markets, although the pressures to act on the information and make improvements might be reduced. One example is what Rosenberg (1982) refers to as 'learning-by-using' in his study in the aircraft industry of the flows of information from user to producer. In competitive markets, both domestic and export, firms will acquire information about the advantages and disadvantages of the products of rivals. Such information might provide the basis for 'learning-by-imitation'. In South Korea, Westphal, Rhee and Pursell (1981) have emphasised the importance of the information feed-back provided by distributors and users to firms in the export sector and Fransman (forthcoming) has examined the importance of imitation for the design of machine tools in Taiwan.

The idea of 'learning-by-doing' has been widely used in the literature in order to capture conceptually the information flows that are generated by the activities of buying, producing, and selling. Corden (1974), for example, thinks of learning-by-doing as an example of joint production, that is, firms produce a stream of output together with a growing stock of capital referred to as knowledge. Earlier Arrow (1962b) and Kaldor (1957) had incorporated the concept in growth models where growth is influenced by some indicator of 'doing', for example, cumulative output or cumulative investment. The concept has also been widely used in the literature on technology in the Third World.

However, there are a number of potential dangers in the incautious use of the notion of learning-by-doing. We have seen that the activities of buying, producing and selling generate flows of new information. However, these flows do not emerge automatically and the quantity and quality of information will be largely dependent on the degree of effort allocated by the firm to facilitate such flows. Furthermore, the improvement-response of individuals and groups within the firm to such information (R & D engineers, production engineers, workers, etc.) is also not automatic but will depend on numerous firm-specific factors. Here it must be kept in mind that change inevitably implies *additional* cost, in terms of the opportunity cost of human and possibly material resources, relative to the no-change situation. The reason is that change requires the acquisition of *new* knowledge. Furthermore, there is always a degree of uncertainty in the process of knowledge acquisition. For these reasons the causal link between 'doing' and, later, changing the ways of doing, is not necessarily a strong one, and is certainly not inevitable.

In the Third World context this point has been forcefully made by Bell, Scott-Kemmis and Satyarakwit (1982) in a study of limited infant industry learning in Thailand, and by Bell, Ross-Larson and Westphal (1984) in an analysis and survey of experience with infant industries in less developed countries.

The lack of an inevitable causal link between new flows of

information, on the one hand, and learning and technical change on the other, raises the question of the conditions necessary to realise the potential improvement made possible by this new information. In turn this brings us back to the earlier discussion of incentives and pressures. In connection with competitive pressures it must be noted that, while they may constitute a powerful 'force' for technical change, they may also be counter-productive if firms are unable, even with an efficient utilisation of the resources at their disposal, to meet such competition successfully. This appears to be the situation, at least in the case of some firms, in the Chilean 'experiment'. In the case of incentives it should be kept in mind that these are only partly financial. Examples illustrating this often forgotten point are Sen's (1983) discussion of Japan in an article entitled 'The Profit Motive', and Rawski's (1978) discussion of technical change in Shanghai mechanical engineering industries prior to the post-1979 reforms in China.

Finally, in discussing the information that 'flows' from the activities of buying, producing and selling and the related concept of learning-by-doing, it is worth counterposing the notion of search. Search has been defined by Nelson and Winter (1982) as 'all those organizational activities which are associated with the evaluation of current routines and which may lead to their modification, to more drastic change, or to their replacement' (p. 400). For present purposes the main difference between the learning-by-doing and search metaphors is that while the former implies a passive role for the firm in the process of technical change and ignores the question of uncertainty, the latter suggests an active role as well as the omnipresence of a greater or lesser degree of uncertainty. In learning-by-doing firms carry out their normal routines and in so doing, automatically accumulate 'knowledge capital'. Search, on the other hand, requires an active intervention, implying both that firms may fail to intervene and that their interventions, when they are undertaken, may be unsuccessful. In view of the failure of the learning-by-doing metaphor to incorporate a satisfactory account of the causal mechanism linking 'doing' and 'learning' (that is, introducing technical change), the search metaphor is generally to be preferred as a way of conceptualising the process of technical change.

Many, but not all, of the flows of information discussed in this section are not mediated by the market mechanism. These externalities have gone largely unnoticed in the literature, probably because the process of technical change itself is so poorly dealt with. Clearly though they are potentially important as indicators of market failure in the area of technical change. However, attention has been given to market-mediated influences on the process of technical change on both the demand and supply sides. In the following two sub-sections we shall consider demand-induced and factor price-induced technical change.

Demand-Induced Technical Change

Here the argument is that innovation is the response to market demand. Among the forms of this argument are the following two: (a) increased, or relatively high, market demand signals profitable opportunities for investment in innovation (see, for example, Schmookler, 1966). (b) Depressed market demand (specifically in the depression phase of the Kondratieff long-wave economic cycle) creates a pressure for firms to innovate and this acts to reduce the lag between basic invention and innovation (Mensch, 1979).

Leaving aside the questions relating to the empirical testing of these hypotheses, several comments may be made about the underlying mechanism of technical change that is suggested. Both arguments posit that changes in demand present signals to firms that will influence their technical change behaviour. (The apparent contradiction between the two views arising from the fact that the first refers to an increase in demand while the latter deals with a reduction in demand is reconciled by seeing changes in both directions as presenting signals that technical change is desirable. However, this is not to suggest that the response to both sets of signals will necessarily be the same. It may well be argued, following our earlier discussion of the asymmetrical effect of incentives and pressures, that reductions in demand will exert a more powerful influence. This indeed is implied in Mensch's argument which sees innovations clustering in the depressive phase of the cycle (with falling or low demand) rather than the upswing (with rising or high demand).)

As Rosenberg (1982: Chapter 10) points out, it is not particularly illuminating to relate changes in demand to an indicator of technical output (such as patents) or the allocation of inventive activity (such as R & D expenditures). The reason is that these magnitudes will simultaneously be influenced by changes on the 'supply' side. The latter include changes in technology, costs, the signals emerging from bottlenecks in production indicating potentially profitable avenues for inventive activity, etc. These 'supply' side factors have to be controlled for in examining the effects of market demand on technical change. At one level the argument that market demand will influence the firm's technological activities is trivial since firms must market their products in order to survive. The real question is the causal significance that is to be attributed to changes in market demand in accounting for variations in technical change behaviour. Exploration of this question requires an examination of the causal significance of the other factors that are simultaneously influencing the same behaviour. In effect it calls for an understanding of the determinants of technical change. As Rosenberg (1982) observes, most studies of the 'demand-induced technical change hypothesis' have failed to examine such determinants, thus implicitly treating firms as 'black boxes' into which demand signals go and out of which technical change comes. Clearly, an acceptable explanation of technical change must go beyond such a treatment of the matter.

A further objection to the 'demand-induced technical change hypothesis' has been made on empirical grounds. Thus Freeman, Clark and Soete (1982) argue that:

a purely demand-led theory of invention and innovation does not correspond to the historical facts in the case of the two technologies which we discuss [synthetic materials and electronics]. Schumpeter's theory of an autonomous impetus on the supply side deriving from advances in science and invention and realized through imaginative entrepreneurship appears to fit the facts rather better. (p. 35)

Rosenberg (1982) makes the same point in the case of semiconductors. However, both sets of authors argue that while the *generation* of new technology may be more 'supply' than demand determined, the *diffusion* of this technology will be to a greater extent demand determined.[14] In the case of Third World countries this observation is important in view of the relatively greater significance of the diffusion, as opposed to the generation, of new technology.

Factor Price-Induced Technical Change

In his *Theory of Wages* (1932) Hicks introduced the notion of technical change being induced by changes in relative factor prices. This idea has been taken up by a number of writers including Ruttan and Hayami (1971) who trace the effects of changing relative resource scarcities and relative prices in agricultural development. Further light is thrown on the question in a retrospective look at the *Theory of Wages* undertaken by Hicks in his Nobel Prize address entitled 'The Mainspring of Economic Growth' (Hicks, 1981). Since this discussion examines not only how firms respond to changing factor prices but also the broader question of the effect of technical change on economic growth, it is worth looking at it briefly here.

Hicks makes it clear that he has two distinct forms of technical change in mind when examining the process of economic growth. The starting point in the story of economic progress is invention. Hicks implies either that 'invention' is exogenous to the economic system, or that if it is endogenous, the determining mechanisms are not adequately understood. However it originates, invention gives an 'impulse' to the economy. As invention is realised in new investment this leads either directly to an increase in output, or, in the case of cost-saving innovations, to indirect increases as resources, freed by the new technique, are absorbed using the old techniques. In the next step in the causal chain, 'rising final output (when it comes) will mean a rising rate of real wages' and therefore 'the rate of profit will decline' (p. 27).

This is where the second form of technical change comes in. As a result of the change in relative factor prices, factor substitution will occur 'along a spectrum of techniques' which will slow the fall in the rate of profit. This is because 'adopting more capital-intensive techniques ... will ... slow up the rise in final product ... [which] will slow up the rise in the rate of real wages' (p. 28). Hicks makes it clear that he sees factor substitution, induced by the change in relative factor prices, in the same light as secondary inventions, the 'children' of the original invention, also induced by the same relative price change. The result of this second form of technical change 'will be to set the economy "aiming" at a steady state with a higher final product per unit of labour, and therefore ... a higher level of wages' (p. 28).

In the Third World context a very similar argument is presented in Little (1982) drawing on the experience of the Asian newly industrialised countries, Hong Kong, Singapore, South Korea and Taiwan. However, the theory of comparative advantage and the consequences of export-oriented policies are integrated into the argument (see Fransman (1984a) for a critical discussion of this and related literature).

Leaving aside other questions relating to Hicks' analysis of the growth process, several brief comments will be made on the role played by technical change. The first is that very little is said about the 'mainspring' which acts as the primary cause in the process of economic growth, the invention which delivers the set of inpulses to the economy. If invention is entirely exogenous to the economic system then the process of economic growth is largely 'at the mercy' of non-economic factors. If, on the other hand, invention is at least partly endogenous then we need to know more about the determining mechanisms. These questions will be taken up in more detail below in the sub-section dealing with science. Second, as we saw earlier, a view which assumes that techniques are 'given' to firms by relative prices (and the assumption of profit-maximisation) may well obscure more than it reveals about the process of technical change. Finally, as mentioned in the previous sub-section, there are many other determinants of technical change and therefore economic growth apart from the influence of changing factor prices. These would also have to be taken into account and their causal significance assessed in any convincing account of the mainsprings of economic growth.

Science
It has been argued that technical change is also determined by an industry's scientific base. However, two opposing hypotheses may be distinguished:

(a) Science-led technical progress. The argument here is that advances in 'fundamental science' create the opportunities for profitable technological applications. This was Schumpeter's view and is largely that of Freeman, Clark and Soete (1982); (b) Economic and technology-led scientific change. Here the view is that science is not autonomous but is influenced by economic incentives and technological trajectories (cf. the argument that the emergence of the steam engine did more for science than the other way round). Thus Rosenberg (1982: Chapter 7) states:

In considering the impact of technology upon science, a central theme of my interpretation is that technological progress plays a very important role in formulating the subsequent agenda for science. The natural trajectory of certain technological improvements identifies and defines the limits of further improvement, which, in turn, focuses subsequent scientific research. (p. 147)

Furthermore, 'Technological progress identifies, in reasonably unambiguous ways, the directions of new scientific research offering a high potential payoff' (p. 148). However, Rosenberg concludes with the 'softer' conclusion that 'the relations between technology and science are ... interactive (and dialectical)' (p. 158).

A similar line of reasoning, although one that stresses the importance of non-economic factors to a greater extent, has been suggested by Constant (1980) and Dosi (1982). They put forward the notion of a technological paradigm analagous to the concept of a scientific paradigm elaborated upon by Kuhn in his *The Structure of Scientific Revolutions* (1962). Closely related is the notion of a technological trajectory, discussed by

Rosenberg (1976) and Nelson and Winter (1977c), which refers to a technological momentum, once a technological paradigm has been selected, which is relatively autonomous from economic determinants.

Relating these arguments to the Third World, much of the research on technology and science institutes has concluded that it is precisely the link from production to technology and science that is absent (see, for example, Herrera, (1973); Cooper, (1973a); and Crane, (1977). It may be suggested, however, that some of this literature has been heavily influenced by dependency theory and accordingly the time may be ripe for a new appraisal of these links.

The State
Since the state encourages, shapes and limits technical change in many important ways, and has had a major impact on the generation of advanced technology and on the diffusion, both national and international, of technology, it is necessary to include the state in any list of sources of technical change. Since, however, a special section below is devoted to this topic the matter is not pursued here.

EXPLAINING TECHNICAL CHANGE

To explain technical change is to reveal the causal mechanisms shaping that change making it assume the form and move in the direction that it does, and preventing it from taking other forms and directions. Since technical change is a complex phenomenon, in the sense that it is brought about by a large number of determining circumstances, its explanation must involve attributing causal significance, or weighting, to each of the circumstances. In practice, as a result of the complexity of technical change, this is extremely difficult to do since it is hard to isolate, and control for, the large number of determinants that simultaneously shape the technical change process. As a result, we presently lack an acceptable explanation that would enable us to account for inter-firm, inter-country and intertemporal differences in the form and direction of technical change. Thus, after an exhaustive survey, Kamien and Schwartz (1982) conclude:

Regardless of which approach is employed, static or dynamic, deterministic or stochastic, decision theoretic or game theoretic, optimizing or behavioural, the quest is for a more complete understanding of the economics of technical advance. As this survey of our present state of knowledge discloses, there is still a long way to go before we can rest. (p. 223)

The absence of an adequate understanding of the causal significance of the factors that shape technical change presents serious problems for empirical work. The reason, as Herbert Simon notes, is that it is impossible in principle to distinguish between real and spurious correlations without some *a priori* assumptions about the causal mechanisms at work.[15] Accordingly, the testing of simple hypotheses regarding the determinants of technical change may not be very revealing in the absence of a satisfactory understanding of the causal mechanisms. The Duhem–Quine thesis is of obvious relevance here.[16] Clearly, therefore, while it may not be possible to search for a complete theory and explanation of technical change as a result of the complexities, it is important to enquire closely into the various causal mechanisms that may shape such change.

EVALUATING TECHNICAL CHANGE

Having examined in this section many of the sources of technical change it is worth briefly concluding with the reminder that, at least for most people, such change is not an end in itself, but rather a means for the fulfilment of other ends. The question is not, therefore, how can 'more' technical change be produced (even assuming that 'we' have a measure of control over technical change — which may not be a justifiable assumption); rather it is how technology can best be used in order to fulfil the ultimate objectives that have been chosen. In answering this question is may well turn out in certain circumstances that a different kind of technology, or even less sophisticated technology, is preferable. For example, in the case of India Lall (1984b) argues that due to government policies a 'great deal of technological effort has gone into socially unproductive uses like finding high-cost local substitutes for imported materials and equipment'. Although the stock of local technological capabilities is increased as a result, it is not clear that such activities are justifiable when judged in terms of the ultimate economic objectives, and in view of the other alternatives that exist.

5 The Capital Goods Sector[17]

INTRODUCTION

The capital goods sector occupies a special role in the technical change process. The reason is that this sector lies at the heart of the processes of technology generation and diffusion. All technical change, whether of the product or process variety, requires the development of modified or new machinery and equipment. Conversely, the diffusion of improved vintages of machinery facilitates the process of technical change in using firms. For this reason the capital goods sector requires special attention in any discussion of technical change.

THE IMPORTANCE OF MACHINERY

Smith and Marx

Although Adam Smith lived in a period before machinery was in widespread use, and although, as Hicks (1965) notes, his basic model was a single period corn model with no important role for fixed capital, he was acutely aware of the significance of machinery. At the beginning of *The Wealth of Nations* Smith singles out machinery as one of the most important contributors to increasing labour productivity. (The other two were 'the increase of dexterity in every particular workman' and 'the saving of the time which is commonly lost in passing from one species of work to another'.) Furthermore, in a number of perceptive remarks, Smith foresaw the emergence of a specialised capital goods sector.

However, of the classical economists it was undoubtedly Karl Marx who provided the most substantial analysis of the development of machinery and its role in accumulation. Of particular importance, as Rosenberg (1982: Chapter 2) points out, is Marx's observation that the introduction of machinery involves the replacement of subjective, human control of the production process by more predictable and controllable natural forces. In this way the conditions were created for the first time for the conscious application of science to production. The cementing of a two-way link between science and production via the development of machinery created the conditions for infinite possibilities for improvement.

Capital-Saving Technical Change

One particular benefit provided by the capital goods sector, as Marx noted, resulted from the development of capital-saving technical change. While in most analyses this form of innovation is usually subordinated to that of labour-saving technical change, capital-saving innovation, as Rosenberg (1976, 1982: passim) observes, has played an important role in facilitating economic growth and increases in product quality.[18]

Total Factor Productivity Growth and Growth Elasticities

There is some evidence in the context of Third World countries to suggest that total factor productivity tends to increase more rapidly in the capital goods sector than in other sectors. This is shown in Table 2 in Nishimizu and Robinson (1983) which shows calculations of total factor productivity in the capital goods sector (non-electrical machinery, electrical machinery and transport equipment) growing on the whole faster than in other sectors in Japan, South Korea and Turkey. Growth elasticities (showing the responsiveness of per capita manufacturing value added to changes in per capita GDP) also tend to be higher in the capital goods sector (similarly defined) than in other sectors as is shown in UNIDO (1979).

Conclusion

For the reasons discussed in this section it is clear that the capital goods sector merits special attention in any consideration of economic growth.

TECHNICAL CHANGE IN THE CAPITAL GOODS SECTOR

In view of the central role played by the capital goods sector in the generation and diffusion of technology and in the process of economic growth, it is worth paying attention to some aspects of technical change in this sector. Of particular concern, relating to the discussion of sources of technical change in the previous section, will be the market and non-market mediated flows of information that facilitate technical change in the capital goods sector. Figure 5.1 forms the basis for the present discussion.

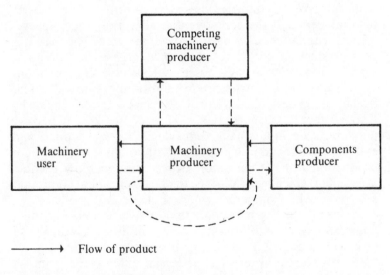

Flow of product

Flow of information

Figure 5.1

The most important function of the capital goods sector lies in the modification, adaptation and innovation of capital equipment. A crucial question, therefore, relates to the acquisition of information on the basis of which capital goods producing firms make these changes. One important source of information, depicted in Figures 1, comes from the interaction between user and producer. Freeman (1974) has shown that information provided by users has been an important factor shaping the kind of technical change produced in the capital goods sector. As Rosenberg (1976) has observed, a unique feature of the capital goods sector follows from the fact that producers of capital goods are often at the same time users of some of the machines that they produce. This is particularly true, for example, in the case of machine tools. As a result, user—producer information flows are to some extent internalised within the firm thus possibly making for a more efficient flow of information and subsequent utilisation of this information for the purposes of technical change. This is shown by the loop in the diagram.

In Third World countries the flow of information from users to producers and the consequential alteration and improvement of capital goods is particularly important. The reason is that production conditions are to a large extent country-specific. In particular, as stressed by Katz (1984b), conditions in Third World countries are in important respects different from those in developed countries. Special mention is made by Katz of factors such as market size, degree of competitive pressure, scale, input quality and availability, factor prices and existing production technique (batch and custom-built production rather than automated continuous-flow production), all of which may influence the kinds of capital goods that are required. Compared to capital goods produced in developed countries in response to the needs of users operating under different conditions in these countries, Third World producers may require, and more profitably use, capital goods that are different in terms of price and quality (for example, functions, precision, durability, size, weight, etc.). An important role, therefore, may be played by a capital goods sector that is able to, and does, respond to the particular needs of local users. Evidence is now accumulating showing, at least for the more industrialised Third World countries, that local capital goods producers are providing capital goods that are significantly different from those available in developed countries. (See, for example, Amsden, 1977, forthcoming; Jacobsson, 1984; Berlinski *et al.*, 1982; and Fransman (1982a, 1984c, forthcoming).

An important role, however, is also played by the suppliers of components who provide information in embodied and disembodied form to, and in turn receive information from, capital goods producers. (See, for example, Cortez (1978) on the role of component suppliers in Argentinian machine production and Fransman (forthcoming) for a discussion of the supply of CNC controls to machine tool producers in Japan and Taiwan.) The importance of the link between component suppliers and capital goods producers raises important questions for government promotion policy.

Finally, account must be taken of the flows of information between competing capital goods producers. While many of the benefits produced by the capital goods sector flow from the economies of specialisation that are reaped in this sector, rather than economies of scale,[19] important advantages are also produced by the interaction between competing firms. As shown in Chudnovsky, Nagao and Jacossson (1984), competing firms often transfer technology to their potential Third World rivals through licensing and other technology agreements. Less studied, however, are the non-market—mediated forms of information and technology transfer that are also important sources of learning and technical change in Third World capital goods producing firms. A particularly important example is the imitation and modification of capital goods produced by developed country competitors. (For an examination of a relatively sophisticated product, CNC machine tools, see Fransman (forthcoming.)

POLICY ISSUES IN THE THIRD WORLD

Of the policy issues that arise in the Third World in connection with the capital goods sector, three will be briefly discussed here: entry into the production of simple capital goods; the make—import decision; and design capabilities.

Entry into Simple Capital Goods
Entry into the production of relatively simple capital goods is fairly easy for most Third World countries. The reason is the 'technological convergence' that Rosenberg (1976) notes exists between the metal-working and machine-producing sectors. In other words, in the case of relatively simple machinery such as some kinds of agricultural machinery or conventional machine tools, the technology, including skills, required to produce the machine is similar to that used in the metal-working sector. For this reason in most Third World countries with a capital goods sector the largest number of firms in the sector originated from the transfer of human and material resources from the metal-working sector. Typically, embryonic capital goods sector firms begin by manufacturing spare parts and components for machinery before moving on to produce complete, but relatively simple, machines. The technological barriers to entry are therefore low and accordingly a relatively large number of firms make the transition.

The Make—Import Decision
For the reasons mentioned thus far, the capital goods sector has a potentially important role to play in the process of economic growth, including quality improvement, in Third World countries. However, while this much can be said, the make—import decision in any particular case may be extremely complex. This is so even in the simplest case where locally produced capital goods are 'cheaper' (that is, in terms of both price and quality) than the imported alternatives in the free trade situation. In this case local users will, by definition, prefer the domestically-produced capital goods and as a result the capital goods sector will grow. This is the situation in Hong Kong examined by Fransman (1982a) where local producers make machines that are simpler in terms of function, less durable and precise, but substantially cheaper than the imported alternatives. These machines are well suited to the

circumstances of relatively small users in South-East Asia who do not have very demanding product quality requirements and as a result the Hong Kong machine-producers studied are also substantial exporters. Accordingly, in Hong Kong the machine-producing sector has grown rapidly despite the existence of free trade in machinery and the absence of selective government promotion, although the sector is smaller relative to manufacturing value added and products tend to be simpler than in other countries such as Singapore, South Korea and Taiwan where governments have selectively intervened to encourage machine production.

But even here complex questions arise. Is there a case for selective government intervention to encourage the production of certain kinds of capital goods that will not be produced in the absence of such intervention? How is this question to be answered in practice? If the answer is in the affirmative, what forms of government intervention are best? On conventional economics grounds externalities, including the information flows referred to earlier and the training of skilled labour, and infant industry learning effects would have to be taken into account although, as is well known, in practice this is extremely difficult to do. These issues are considered in more detail below in the section dealing with infant industries and the state. There it is shown that the governments of many of the more industrialised Third World countries have intervened to promote the capital goods sector using policies that conventional economic theory would tend to suggest are non-optimal. Furthermore, they have not attempted to justify, or argue for, their interventions on the basis of either prior or subsequent quantitative analyses of the externalities and learning effects.

The Design and Production of Complex Capital Goods
In order to be able to fulfil the function of adapting, modifying and innovating capital goods, producers require design capabilities. The bigger the changes, the more sophisticated are the design capabilities that are necessary. At the most sophisticated extreme, knowledge of the underlying scientific principles will be required.

A recent study by Chudnovsky, Nagao and Jacobsson (1984) of capital goods producers in Brazil, India and South Korea concludes that the design capabilities of the most sophisticated producers in these countries are still relatively limited. Examining these results, Chudnovsky (1985) concludes that:

the evidence is far from conclusive about the progress made by firms surveyed in mastering design and manufacturing technology. All firms rely on licensors for design technology and most of them have not been able as yet to use licensing agreements to learn design methodology. One reason is the reluctance of licensors to provide recent designs .... [B]asic design and, in some cases, even detailed designs for complex capital goods are not yet mastered by leading producers in the countries studied. Accordingly, they suffer from a major handicap which affects their ability to fulfil their role as eventual generators of technological innovations.

More research is needed, however, on the precise factors which constrain the development of design capabilities in Third World countries.

6 Changing Paradigms

One of the main themes of this article has been the increasing interest in the forms of technical change originating *within* Third World countries. However, in this section, it will be suggested that the shift in focus was not simply the result of a process of 'internal evolution' within research programmes. Rather, it will be argued, changes in *theoretical paradigms* played a crucial role in changing the conceptual perspective. More specifically, it will be suggested that four sets of factors combined to produce the change. These were: the decline of dependency theory; the decline of neoclassical theory; the rise of the newly-industrialised (or semi-industrial) countries, particularly the four in Asia (Hong Kong, Singapore, South Korea and Taiwan); and the emergence of a new paradigm that is best labelled neo-Schumpeterian.

Some idea of the importance of theoretical paradigm is obtained by rereading the literature on technological dependence of the early to mid-1970s, from the perspective of the mid-1980s. In this literature some writers put forward what might currently be thought of as a 'hard' or 'rigid' view of technological dependence as the following quotation from Cardoso makes clear:

Basically the dependence situation is maintained because, in addition to the already stated factors of direct control by the multinationals and dependence on the external markets, the industrial sector develops in an incomplete form. The production goods sector (Department 1), which is the centre-pin of accumulation in a central economy, does not develop fully. Ordinarily, economists refer to 'technological dependency' and it means that the economy has to import machines and industrial inputs, and consequently has to stimulate exports (especially of primary goods) to generate the necessary foreign exchange. (Quoted in Warren, 1980: 181–2)

The conclusions of the 'rigid' view, however, were by no means confined to those who lacked an understanding of the history and complexity of technological change, as the following quotation from the astute Rosenberg shows:

Many of the major innovations in Western technology have emerged in the capital goods sector of the economy. But underdeveloped countries with little or no organized domestic capital goods sector simply have not had the opportunity to make capital-saving innovations because they have not had the capital goods industry necessary for them. Under these circumstances, such countries have typically imported their capital goods from abroad, but this has meant that they have not developed the technological base of skills, knowledge, facilities and organization upon which further technical progress so largely depends. (1976: 146–7)[20]

By the end of the 1970s, however, a somewhat 'softer' view of technological dependency was widely in vogue as Sen's (1980) statement makes clear:

The technological dependence of the developing countries on the developed areas has received a great deal of attention in recent years. The peculiar feature of this dependence is its asymmetry. An interdependence that operates mutually does not entail a subservient role for either side. However, the technological dependence that exists currently is not of that kind and reflects the dominant role of one group of countries as suppliers of modern technology and the dominated role of another group as mere receivers. (pp. 133–4)

However, there were in the mid-1970s also those who, while basically adhering to this 'softer' view were cautious about some of the conclusions that might be drawn from a 'rigid' perspective. Among them was Lall who, significantly, was also one of the first to turn attention to the importance of technical progress in the more industrialised Third World countries. In an influential article Lall (1975) noted:

A number of dependent economies have demonstrated an ability ... to break out of the constricting circle predicted by dependency ... theorists .... The interesting problems to investigate ... are those concerning why some LDCs are able to successfully integrate themselves into a dynamic capitalist trade system and others are not .... A blanket concept of dependence applied to all LDCs is quite misleading. (p. 12)

There is a similar note of ambivalence in Stewart's (1977) chapter entitled 'Technological Dependence'. While noting that 'In most of this chapter we shall be concentrating on the undesirable consequences of technological dependence', Stewart added:

The transfer of technology from advanced countries has enabled countries in the Third World to benefit from the manifold developments of science and technology in the industrialized countries ... without themselves going through the difficult and costly process of developing it. This is one of the main advantages of being a 'late-comer' in terms of development ... the advantages ... may explain why a country may be justified in pursuing a policy of technology transfer and hence permitting the associated technological dependence despite the considerable costs so incurred. (p. 122)

By the late 1970s, however, the 'rigid' dependency view showed signs of becoming what Lakatos refers to as a 'degenerating scientific research programme'. The 'hard core' of this programme, containing amongst others the view that indigenous technological development was impossible as a result of the unavoidable reliance of Third World countries on imported technology, seemed increasingly to be untenable. In large part, the dependency programme's degeneracy was attributable to its inability to explain, as noted in the above quotation from Lall (1975) the apparent economic success of a number of more industrialised Third World countries.

Research done in the later 1970s by Katz and Lall on Latin America and India, and a little later by Westphal, Rhee and Pursell on South Korea, showed that countries such as these were able to successfully master foreign technology and use it for exports; and that important, though incremental, forms of technical change were occurring in these countries, resulting in the export of modified products and processes. These forms of technical change contributed to the rapid growth in output and manufactured exports from these countries. With the under-mining of the 'rigid' view of technological dependence there emerged an increasing theoretical predisposition to 'see' technological change occurring in the Third World.[21]

At the same time, dependency theory was also under attack from orthodox Marxists, some of whom, like Warren (1980), saw the rise of the newly industrialised Third World countries as confirming the view that Marx expressed so clearly in the *Manifesto* (even though it was less consistent with the views of Lenin and other communists on the effects of imperialism):

The bourgeoisie cannot exist without constantly revolutionizing the instruments of production and thereby the relations of production; and with them the whole relations of society. Conservation of the old modes of production in an altered form was, on the contrary, the first condition of existence of all earlier industrial classes. Constant revolutionizing of production, uninterrupted disturbance of all social conditions, everlasting uncertainty, and agitation distinguish the bourgois epoch from all earlier ones. The bourgeoisie ... draw all, even the most barbarian nations into civilization. The cheap prices of its commodities are the heavy artillery with which it batters down all Chinese walls.... It compels all nations, on pain of extinction, to adopt the bourgeois mode of production.... In a word *it creates a world after its own image.* (Marx and Engels, 1984, emphasis added)[22]

These views, put forward in books such as Warren's provocatively titled *Imperialism: Pioneer of Capitalism* (1980), further undermined the 'rigid' dependency view. With the demise of 'rigid' dependency theory, the way was further opened for an examination of technical change in the Third World.

Research on technology in the Third World was also greatly influenced by the neoclassical paradigm in economics. We saw earlier that much of this research focused on neoclassical-type questions such as: the labour and capital intensity of technology, the substitutability of labour and capital in response to changing factor prices, and the use of shifts in an aggregate production function in order to estimate the contribution of 'technical change' to output and productivity. While the neoclassical paradigm certainly did throw some light on the question of technical change, some writers, like Nelson and Winter (1982), began in the 1970s to express the view that it too had become a degenerating research programme:

Following upon the discovery that there was a large 'residual' involved in neo-classical explanations of economic growth, and the identification of that residual with technical change, economists undertook a considerable amount of research aimed toward pinning down what technical change actually is . . . . But what we now know about technical change should not be comforting to an economist who has been holding the hypothesis that technical change can be easily accommodated within an augmented neo-classical model. Nor can the problem here be brushed aside as involving a phenomenon that is 'small' relative to those that are well handled by the theory; rather it relates to a phenomenon [that is, technical change] that all analysts (or virtually all) acknowledge as the central one in economic growth. The tail now wags the dog. And the dog does not fit the tail very well. The neo-classical approach to growth theory has taken us down a smooth road to a dead end. (pp. 204–5)

Thus, quite apart from the so-called capital controversy, the neoclassical paradigm was weakened by its inability to come to grips with the determinants of technical change. Indeed, Nelson (1981) has suggested that 'the canonical neoclassical formulation not merely over-simplifies but obscures some of the central factors of productivity growth' (p. 1035).[23] With the fall from dominance of the neoclassical paradigm the possibility of new approaches to the question of technical change was enhanced.[24]

But what are the features of these 'new approaches'? One perspective which appears to be in the process of becoming dominant in the Third World context may appropriately be labelled neo-Schumpeterian. Although this approach emphasises incremental as well as major technical change, contrasting with Schumpeter's exclusive concern with the latter, its other features are truer to the original Schumpeter.

The neo-Schumpeterian approach is concerned above all with the process of economic change, as opposed to the analysis of equilibrium states. Central to the process of economic change is technical change, initiated by the entrepreneur in the earlier Schumpeterian view, or by the R & D departments of larger firms in the later view.[25] Firms use technical change, improving products and processes, as a major weapon in the competitive struggle, either taking the offensive and introducing innovations, or defending their positions by jumping on the bandwagon and imitating their successful rivals. The result is a continual series of disequilibria as change and adjustment to change occur. In the neo-Schumpeterian approach uncertainty is also central. The outcome of investment in technical change is uncertain; different firms have differing views as to the best prospects; some firms succeed and grow, others decline and sink. The process of economic growth is the sum total of all these events.

Few attempts have been made to formalise the neo-Schumpeterian approach (with the notable exception of the simulation models constructed by Nelson and Winter in their 'evolutionary' approach), and few would claim that it offers at present an adequate explanation of technical change. The neo-Schumpeterian approach is possibly most appropriately seen as being in a 'pre-paradigmatic' stage of its development. In other words, while certain central aspects of the technical change process have been identified, these together with other economic, sociopolitical and cultural aspects have not yet been rigorously welded into an acceptable theory of the determinants of technical change. Whether such a theory is indeed possible in view of the complexity of the process of technical change is a serious question. However, it cannot be doubted that the neo-Schumpeterian approach is currently beginning to yield a rich stream of case-study material.[26]

7 Developed Country Technology: Opportunity or Constraint?

In recent years there has been a renewed interest in the net benefits arising from the international diffusion of technology. Such diffusion has, of course, long been of central importance. Thus, as Rosenberg (1982: Chapter 11) notes, the three great inventions which Francis Bacon suggested 'changed the whole face and state of things throughout the world', namely, printing, gunpowder and the compass, originated, not in Europe, but in China. However, it would appear that there are at least two related reasons for the current increase in interest in the international diffusion of technology. The first is the paradox inherent in changes in world technological leadership. Such changes are paradoxical since there are many reasons (some of which are summarised in Myrdal's notion of cumulative causation) to expect that the world technology leader will maintain, and even increase, its lead. Technology-related reasons include the country's experience generated at the technology frontier, its monopolisation, to a greater or lesser extent, of the knowledge it has generated, and its economic gains from the sale of technology and goods embodying superior technology. Yet history has shown that international technology leadership has been difficult to sustain over extended periods of time. Thus, for example, Ranis (1977) notes that:

in spite of all efforts to keep advances in technology 'bottled up' in

65

the British Isles, through prohibiting the export of workers before 1825 and of machinery before 1842, by the time of the Crystal Palace Exhibition in 1851 there were clear indications that the Continent, especially Germany, was taking the lead in the important chemical, pharmaceutical, and electrical engineering industries, with the United States forging ahead in mechanical engineering. (p. 6)

Similar examples in the current period of Japanese firms either catching up or overtaking the world leaders occur with such frequency that further mention of them is unnecessary. The second reason for interest in international diffusion is the rise of the newly-industrialised countries which have been able to grow and export rapidly with a comparatively meagre technological infrastructure.

Clearly, it is one thing to observe 'catch up' and changes in world technology leadership, but quite another to explain it. Nevertheless, there is an emerging consensus in the literature that there are important advantages in a firm or country being a technology follower. Most importantly, the costs of knowledge and risk are reduced, thus facilitating increases in productivity at relatively little cost. This relates closely to the 'depth of knowledge' discussion above, suggesting that only relatively 'shallow' levels of knowledge are required in adopting a technology-following position behind the world technology leader(s). Thus W.A. Lewis (1957) has stated that:

it is not necessary to be a pioneer in order to have a large export trade. It is sufficient to be a quick imitator. Britain would have done well enough if she merely imitated German and American innovations. Japan, Belgium and Switzerland owe more of their success as exporters of manufactures to imitation than they do to innovation.

Similarly, in discussing the fact that in the 1950s and 1960s, while the United States and Britain had the highest ratio of R & D spending to gross national product, they had the lowest rates of productivity growth, Nelson and Langlois (1983) conclude:

part of the message seems to be that it matters where a country is relative to the frontier of technology and productivity. Countries not on the frontier can 'play catch up' fairly easy without much R & D spending so long as their rates of physical investment are high. Countries nearer the frontier have to work harder for each percentage increase in productivity. This begins to suggest that it is not necessarily to a country's great advantage to be alone on the frontier. (p. 815)

Emphasising that only 'relatively low' levels of knowledge are necessary in the earlier stages of industrialisation, Westphal, Rhee and Pursell (1981) have stated that South Korea's

technological mastery has progressed much further in plant operation than in plant and product design. It thus appears that the know-how to operate production processes efficiently is, to a large degree, independent of the ability to use the underlying engineering principles in investment activity .... That is not to deny that ... Koreans have become increasingly involved in various phases of project implementation. Nonetheless, it is not too great an overstatement to say that Korea has become a significant industrial power simply on the basis of efficiency in production.

However, 'catch up' on the basis of foreign technology is not merely a passive process for the recipient country. As we saw earlier, and as Rosenberg (1982) emphasises, 'perhaps the most distinctive single factor determining the success of technology transfer is the early emergence of an indigenous technological capacity' (p. 271). It will be seen later that a central feature of Japan's successful assimilation of foreign technology lay in the measures taken to minimise foreign control and maximise the development of local technological capabilities consequent on the import of technology, thus facilitating adaptation and improvement processes. However, Rosenberg (1982) has suggested that the kinds of capabilities required by the currently dominant 'technological paradigms' (see Dosi (1982) and Freeman, Clark and Soete (1982) for an elaboration of this concept) are qualitatively different from those necessary in the nineteenth century.

An increasing number of industrial technologies are becoming science-based, a situation strikingly different from the nineteenth century .... [Accordingly] it may become increasingly difficult to borrow or imitate without a reasonably high-level domestic science capability .... If this turns out to be so, it may be important in slowing down the progression of the less industrial countries to increasingly complex, research-intensive production. (p. 277)

However, even here the constraints are not absolute, contrary to what is suggested by a 'rigid' dependency view. One reason is that 'The life-cycle of many products demonstrates that, as even high-technology products mature and stabilise, new possibilities emerge that make their production more compatible with the relative factor prices and skills available in less advanced economies' (ibid). Incremental, rather than basic designing skills, may play a central role: 'there seem to be many opportunities for modifications in final product design or specification that will make high-technology products far more compatible with the capabilities of less advanced economies' (ibid). A case in point is the 'Apple-like' personal computers manufactured and sold at low price in Hong Kong and Taiwan.[27]

One conceptual implication of this discussion is that the rigid distinction between 'diffusion' and 'generation' of technology is inappropriate, since technologies are modified, adjusted and improved upon in the process of their diffusion. Thus, whereas previous studies tended to examine the diffusion of a technology assumed to be unchanging (see, for example, Mansfield's studies of diffusion), the recognition of the cumulative significance of incremental improvements requires that the processes of diffusion and technical change need to be conceptually linked.[28] It may well be that part of the reason for Japan's successful 'catch up' and, in some cases, 'take over' lies in the technical change generated by rapid diffusion which was itself facilitated by appropriate socio-political relations and fuelled by high rates of investment.

This discussion suggests that it may be illuminating to distinguish between two different 'ideal type' technology strategies (for firms, industries or countries): (a) attempting to reach the world technology frontier, that is, the 'catch up' strategy; and (b) using, but not attempting, even in the long run, to generate frontier technology, that is, the 'frontier following' strategy. Although circumstances differ from industry to industry within each country, it may be possible to associate various countries with these two strategies without doing undue violence to the facts. Thus, as Ranis (1977) points out in the above quotation, Germany and the United States followed the 'catch up' strategy in the nineteenth century. The two outstanding examples of this strategy in the twentieth century are Japan and, in more restricted areas, the Soviet Union. While Japan benefited from the international diffusion of technology, it seems that firms explicitly aimed to produce *better* products than the world leaders. In most cases the improvements were of an incremental nature, using Western technology as a starting point, and did not (at least until quite recently) involve Japanese-produced major innovations. Peck and Tamura (1976) distinguish between improvement, adaptation and cost-reduction as three distinct objectives in Japanese incremental technical change. Referring to a 1962 Ministry of International Trade and Industry (MITI) study they note that 'one-third of R & D expenditures ... were for modifying or improving imported technology' (p. 542). Such expenditures 'have often been viewed as adaptive research, implying that the objective is to modify the technology for Japanese conditions'. However, on the basis of their own interviews Peck and Tamura suggest

that 'improvement engineering' may be the better description. The emphasis was, first of all, on quality control *with the goal being to exceed the product quality of the foreign manufacturer....* A second, lower priority was to improve the product in terms of operating simplicity, attractiveness, and technical performance .... Cost reduction ... was given a lower priority. (pp. 542–3, emphasis added)

Despite the problems of productivity slow-down referred to by Nelson and Langlois (1983) above, the Japanese example shows that there are substantial rewards for a country that succeeds in reaching the technology frontier in some areas. These rewards stem largely from the country's international competitive position. However, as we saw, Lewis (1957) has pointed out that smaller European countries like Belgium and Switzerland have successfully pursued a 'frontier following' strategy. Newly industrialised countries like Hong Kong and Taiwan consciously pursue similar policies, without attempting to reach the frontier.

However, there are extremely difficult problems that are confronted in following these strategies. Some of these will be discussed briefly here. A major problem in the 'catch up' strategy is the initial selection, by private firms and/or by the state, of the industries that are to be developed. Clearly, not all industries will merit development since in some cases the long-run costs will obviously outweigh the associated long-run benefits. The problem of selection is all the more difficult since, by definition, the industry will be inefficient in the short run compared to international best practice. This difficulty has been precisely described by a Vice-Minister of the Japanese MITI:

The Ministry of International Trade and Industry decided to establish in Japan industries which require intensive employment of capital and technology, industries that in consideration of competitive cost of production should be the most inappropriate for Japan, industries such as steel, oil refining, petrochemicals, automobiles, aircraft, industrial machinery of all sorts, and electronics including electronic computers. From a short-run static viewpoint, encouragement of such industries would seem to conflict with economic rationalism. But, from a long-range viewpoint, these are precisely the industries where income elasticity of demand is high, technological progress is rapid, and labour productivity rises fast. (OECD, 1972: 92)

The conflict between short-run and long-run criteria implied in this quotation presents serious problems for technology and investment analysis. Most techniques of investment analysis such as social cost-benefit analysis and empirical measurements of comparative advantage like the domestic resource cost of foreign exchange are essentially static. The problem with dynamic calculations, however, is that they are subject to a significant degree of uncertainty. With hindsight we know that

Japanese long-run calculations were correct in many industries; however, from an *ex ante* perspective, such as that confronting a country contemplating following a 'catch up' strategy, the problem is fundamentally more complicated.[29] We shall return to this issue in the following section dealing with infant industries.

Another problem in following the 'catch up' strategy lies in deciding on correct 'sequencing' in developing 'deeper' levels of knowledge[30] in the industries that have been selected. It has been suggested, as was pointed out above, that in the earlier stages of industrialisation, and possibly of the 'catch up' process, only relatively 'low' levels of knowledge are required. The case of Japan, Ranis (1977, 1984) argues, was characterised by a progression from simpler production engineering skills through more complicated applied research to, more recently, basic research, rather than the other way round.[31] Costs increase as progression takes place to 'deeper' levels of knowledge. However, the 'sequencing' problem is complex since in some instances 'deeper' knowledge levels may be required in order to facilitate routine production with 'lower' levels of knowledge. This is implied in Rosenberg's (1982) statements above on the science-based nature of newer industrial activities in areas such as electronics and on the need for (incremental rather than basic) design skills. While in principle an investment in 'deeper' knowledge should be subject to a cost-benefit calculation, in practice this calculation is usually rather *ad hoc* as a result of the uncertainties.

The 'technology following' strategy differs from the 'catch up' strategy in that it attempts to use foreign knowledge efficiently *without* in the longer run building up the capabilities to challenge the frontier leaders. Selection of industries will take place with this in mind. The strategy does not preclude the selection of infant industries that, it is hoped, will become internationally efficient with the passage of time. Investment in knowledge and knowledge-creating capabilities will be undertaken with the aim of utilising foreign knowledge most productively. Foreign knowledge will be 'imported' in various forms utilising both market and non-market processes such as direct foreign investment, licensing and other know-how agreements, imitation, scanning of foreign trade journals, learning-by exporting, etc. 'Technology following' will often involve situations where the frontier is stagnant or shifting outwards only slowly, or alternatively, where earlier vintage techniques are used which are not currently employed in more highly industrialised countries. More complicated will be the case where the frontier is moving rapidly and the problem is one of 'keep up' rather than 'catch up'. In turn this raises many difficult problems and the question of investment in knowledge will also be central. For a case study that delves into some of these issues in an examination of the Taiwanese machine tool industry see Fransman (forthcoming).

In following both strategies, a central analytical and policy problem will arise in evaluating the longer-run social costs and benefits of technological self-reliance in selected areas, given the alternative of importing technology. While in principle self-reliance is only justifiable where the long-run social benefits outweigh the associated costs, it will often be difficult from an *ex ante* point of view to establish whether this criterion is met. In the case of India, however, Lall (1984b) suggests that in some areas 'self-reliant' technological change has not resulted in internationally efficient products and processes even with the passage of long periods of time, and other examples are to be found in Bell (1982). Since the possibility of importing technology exists, it will accordingly be necessary to enquire whether it is more efficient *in the long run* to transform domestic resources directly into locally generated technology (also taking externalities into account), or to change them into technology indirectly through exporting to earn foreign exchange, and consequently foreign technology. *In this connection it must be kept in mind, as discussed earlier, that importing technology, and generating technology domestically, are usually not mutually exclusive alternatives.* As a result of the 'implicitness' of imported technology referred to by Nelson, numerous small problems will have to be solved by the importer and these will require an indigenous technological capability. Similarly, domestically-generated 'self-reliant' technology will frequently require imported inputs.

However, while arguments about the substantial net benefits to be gained from the international diffusion of technology are largely based on the Japanese experience, some, like Cooper (1980), have suggested that 'there may be some doubts about the applicability of Japanese experience to other countries' (p. 7)[32] Others such as Kaplinsky (1984c), Hoffman and Rush (1980) and Hoffman (1981) have argued that recent 'leaps' in the technology frontier as a result of microelectronic applications have made the 'catch up' or 'technology following' strategies more difficult, if not impossible to pursue. The complexity of microelectronics-based systems, it is argued, makes it hard for less industrialised countries to follow suit. As Kaplinsky (1984c) puts it:

the assertion that LDCs can continue to assimilate DC technology at an unchanged rate, that they can continue their penetration of DC markets in increasingly technology-intensive manufactures, must be open to question. In contrast I offer a view that suggests that the gap between DC and LDC technology is reopening, but at the same time DC technology is becoming increasingly inappropriate for LDCs. (p. 158)

Time will tell whether the constraints are as binding as Kaplinsky and Hoffman suggest, but at the very least the case studies that they refer to (ranging from CAD/CAM systems to textile automation) point to the difficulties of catching up and following in the face of major technological changes. However, others such as Soete (1983) and Stewart (1984) have argued that at least the newly industrialised countries may be in a strong position to absorb the new technologies thus differentiating themselves even more from the rest of the Third World.

8 Infants, Exports and Technical Progress

INFANT INDUSTRY PROTECTION

An interest in the question of infant industries goes back in the history of economic thought to writers such as Adam Smith and John Stuart Mill.[33] However, in the development economics literature there has recently been a renewed interest in infant industries. There are three related reasons, it would appear, for this rebirth of interest.[34]

First and foremost is the realisation that neoclassical trade and industry theory, based as it is on a conceptual framework of static resource allocation, does not provide an adequate explanation of growth in output and productivity. This is noted by Krueger, a notable neoclassical economist who edited one of the major studies on the export-promoting countries (Krueger, 1978). In considering the relationship between free trade, exports and economic growth, Krueger (1981) observes that 'At first glance the superiority of the export-promotion strategy appeared to vindicate the view of trade theorists, who had advocated free trade and who saw export promotion as coming closer to a free trade regime than did import substitution' (p. 3). However,

the simple 2 × 2 comparative advantage model would seem to suggest that growth rates would be the same under autarky and under free trade, once the once-and-for-all losses associated with accepting a

75

non-optimal trade policy are absorbed. Thus, there are no theorems from standard trade theory with regard to the effect on the growth rate of departures from optimal trade policy. (p. 6)

Second, and related to the first point, is the realisation that economic policy in many of the rapidly growing newly-industrialised countries, in particular South Korea which has become something of a 'test case', has departed significantly from the central neoclassical policy prescriptions. Several examples will serve to illustrate this. To begin with, in attempting to explain the superior economic performance of the so-called outward-oriented, as opposed to the inward-oriented, countries it has often been argued that a major reason is the absence in the former countries of a bias in the incentive system against exports and primary activities. Balassa's conclusion (Balassa and Associates, 1982) represents this view. With reference to the better performance of South Korea, Singapore and Taiwan, Balassa argues that these countries 'avoided a bias against exports and primary activities, provided broadly equal incentives to most exports ... ensured the stability of the incentive system [and] had the best export performance' (p. 59). However, on closer inspection, far from avoiding a bias against exports and primary activities, the South Korean state has discriminated *in favour* of these activities in the export sector. This emerged in important studies of effective rates of protection and effective subsidies by Westphal and Kim (1977) and Chong Hyun Nam (1981). It may be that these magnitudes do not provide an adequate indication of prevailing incentives.[35] Nevertheless according to Chong Hyun Nam's figures 'the relative incentives accorded to the manufacturing sector, which accounted for nearly 90 per cent of exports in 1978, reveal that export sales, on average, receive greater incentives than domestic sales, with 16 per cent effective incentives for export sales versus four per cent protection for domestic sales' (p. 205).

In commenting on the 16 per cent figure, Corden states: 'This figure seems surprisingly low .... It would not be surprising if an alternative calculation yielded a figure of perhaps 30 percent' (Corden, 1981: 212). The effective subsidies for exports are largely the result of the ready availability of credit at substantially below market rates of interest (see Chong Hyun Nam, 1981: 195, for details). However, South Korea's export-bias presents a dilemma for conventional trade theory, as Findlay (1981) pointed out:

In terms of the standard theory of trade and welfare, a bias in favour of exports is no better in principle than a bias against them.... In comparison with the optimal free trade level a 'right wing deviation' in trade policy that discriminates in favour of exports is not better than the equivalent 'left wing deviation' that discriminates in favour of import substitution. It is therefore hard to see why an export-promotion strategy should produce such successful results, since both types of bias are equally to be condemned from the standpoint of static allocative efficiency. (p. 31)

Furthermore, the South Korean system of incentives is also industry-biased. Yet, as Westphal (1981) notes, the conventional view is that 'though modest levels of promotional incentives to infant industries may be in order, the closer is the policy regime to free trade, the better is the industrial performance, because a free trade regime necessarily means uniformity of incentives *vis-à-vis* trading opportunities' (p. 1). While under free trade incentives are by definition uniform, a uniformity of effective protection is usually held to be preferable to 'made-to-measure' effective protection. The reasoning is supplied by Corden (1980):

The essential idea of uniformity is that the same rates of protection be provided for all activities in manufacturing so that there is no discrimination other than that which comes naturally out of the price system.... Thus, as far as possible, the principle of comparative advantage is applied. This, indeed, is the main advantage of the uniformity approach. (p. 72)

Furthermore, it is usually argued that only modest levels of uniform protection are justifiable. However, parts of the South Korean economy have been selectively protected at high rates of effective protection although, as we shall shortly see, exports have also been important from these sectors. Chong Hyun Nam notes that 'despite the import liberalization attempts since the early 1960s, most of the import— substitution industries are still highly protected by various import controls' (1981: 187). In effect 'there seems to have been little if any overall import liberalization during the period 1968–78' (p. 202). While the effective rate of protection in 1978 for the manufacturing sector as a whole was relatively low at 5.3 per cent (Balassa method), this aggregate figure conceals wide variations. Furthermore, the high rates of effective protection were not confined to the so-called heavy industrial sectors (the development of which has been criticised as a result of its capital- and foreign-exchange intensity by Little (1982: 11, 146, 241; 1979: 32) and Lal (1983: 45–8). The effective rate of protection in 1978 for the five most heavily protected sectors of the economy were as follows: transport equipment—135 per cent (mainly ships: South Korea has now become a major world exporter of ships); consumer durables—131 per cent; agriculture, forestry and fishing—77 per cent; machinery 47 per cent; and non-durable consumer goods—32 per cent (Nam, 1981).

Moreover, the method chosen for protecting South Korean infant industry also conflicts with what is generally prescribed by conventional theory. This theory suggests that subsidies are to be preferred, followed by tariffs and quantitative restrictions on the grounds that the correct use of the former instrument comes closest to correcting distortions at their source. As Corden (1980) notes:

If the objective is to expand manufacturing on grounds of protecting infant industries, a tariff and set of import quotas is clearly not optimal. Compared with a direct subsidy to manufacturing output, it creates a consumption distortion by unnecessarily shifting the pattern of domestic demand away from manufactures. In addition, it creates a home-market bias by failing to protect exports of manufactures. The latter distortion could be eliminated by supplementing the tariff with export subsidies. (p. 64)

However, as Westphal (1981) has pointed out, in South Korea

'"tailor-made" infant industry protection has typically been afforded via quantitative restrictions on imports' (p. 16). (In Japan, too, industries selected for development 'were afforded the protection of high tariff and quantitative import controls' as Allen (1981: 90) observes.) Moreover, 'Infant industries in Korea begin exporting—both directly and indirectly—at a very early stage, often at once, notwithstanding that these sales do not receive subsidies sufficient to offset the absolute protection that is granted only to non-export-related sales' (Westphal, 1981: 25).

Accordingly, contrary to the prescriptions of conventional theory, parts of the Korean economy exhibit an export bias in the incentive system, while other selected sectors have been given extremely high rates of effective protection with quantitative import restrictions as the preferred policy instrument. As Westphal (1981) notes, this policy has been successful in the South Korean case:

It is not my purpose to inquire why most governments appear to favour protection as the principal instrument of infant industry promotion or to argue that they are correct in this respect. Instead, I simply want to establish that infant industry protection can 'work' in the sense of fostering the rapid achievement of internationally competitive levels of productivity. (p. 16)

Hence it would appear that the experience of countries like South Korea and possibly Brazil (if not the prior example of Japan) has provided a powerful reason for the closer investigation of infant industry experience in the Third World.[36]

A third, and closely related reason for the renewed interest in infant industries is that, as Krueger (1981) points out, in contrast to 'the static optimality of free trade', the 'infant industry case for departures from free trade is based squarely on a presumed dynamic effect' (p. 6). In his careful study Corden (1974) divides these into dynamic internal and external economies. In a situation where, as we saw earlier, conventional trade theory is unable to make predictions about the effect on growth of alternative trade regimes, the chance to come to grips with the dynamic factors affecting productivity and growth through the study of infant industries is obviously attractive.

For these reasons the study of infant industries has once again been placed firmly on the research agenda. But when is it justified to extend infant industry protection? Formally this can be illustrated in Figure 8.1, taken from Bell (1982) and Bell, Ross-Larson and Westphal (1983).

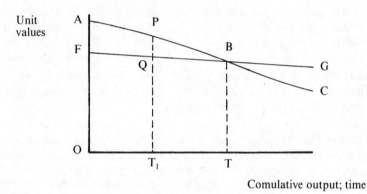

Figure 8.1

OA represents the initial unit cost of infant production measured in the appropriate shadow prices. ABC shows falling unit costs as productivity increases. OF is the unit cost of importing the product measured at the relevant shadow price of foreign exchange, while FG shows the path of unit import costs. FAB is the total undiscounted cost of infancy while CBG represents the total benefit. The net benefit is obtained by applying an appropriate time—discount rate to the total costs and benefits. With time measured along the horizontal axis, OT represents the duration of infancy.

Several things should be noted about this diagram. The first is that it is not always necessary for infant industries to be protected. See Corden (1974) for a discussion of the conditions under which infant industry protection is justified. Second, when AC refers to an individual firm, it does not reflect the externalities generated by the firm. These would have to be added in the calculation of total benefits. These externalities may be important and include labour training, knowledge diffusion and the creation of an atmosphere conducive to productivity increase as discussed in Corden (1974). Third, the conditions for infant industry investment may not be as strenuous as appears in the diagram. Once allowance is made for product quality differences, the scope is widened for Third World countries to become 'internationally efficient' in particular areas (for example, the production of cheaper, lower-quality machinery particularly suited to Third World conditions).

What determines the slope and shape of AC and therefore, with a given FG, the duration of infancy? Bell *et al.* suggest that while many factors, both external and internal to the firm, will influence changes in productivity and therefore the time path of unit costs, it is the firm's own technological capabilities and efforts which are central. In general this will require the conscious allocation of resources; the 'automatic' accretion of experience as a function of time will not exert a significant effect on productivity. However, while Bell (1982) points to the serious shortcomings in the available research, it is clear that there is a wide variance in the duration of infancy in the cases that have been studied. On the one hand are the successful cases such as the USIMINAS steel plant in Brazil studied by Dahlman and Fonseca (1978) where total factor productivity more than doubled in a period of seven years. Drawing on this and other South Korean cases Westphal (1981) concluded that 'it may not be exceptional for the unit domestic resource cost of production in a particular type of activity to fall at an annual rate of around ten per cent during the first five to ten years of production' (p. 9). However, while this may not be exceptional, Bell, Ross-Larson and Westphal (1983) suggest that it is far from the experience of most infant industries in most Third World countries:

We ... draw only two reasonably clear conclusions. First, productivity growth in infant industries appears to be highly variable, even in apparently similar economic conditions. Second, few of the infant enterprises studied in less developed economies appear to have demonstrated the high and continuous productivity growth needed to achieve and maintain international competitiveness. (p. 22)

We do know that infants can mature. Moreover, the experience in some rapidly industrializing countries suggests that they can even mature very quickly. But reflecting our general ignorance of the maturation process, there is little general agreement on the factors ultimately responsible for the rapid maturation in these countries. (p. 39)

One hypothesis that has been put forward with reference to the case of South Korea, is that this country's 'selectively protected infant industries exhibit superior performance as a result of their export activity' (Westphal, 1981: 35).[37] This hypothesis has recently derived some empirical support from a study by Nishimizu and Robinson (1983). It raises the intriguing possibility that infant industries are most effective, not as part of import-substitution policies as was originally thought, but rather under an export-oriented regime.

There are several reasons for suggesting that exporting activities will result in positive effects on total factor productivity. The first is the competitive pressures that are brought to bear on exporters to improve product quality and reduce cost. Second, there are the opportunities for international inter-firm learning that are opened up by exporting activities which have been stressed by Westphal, Rhee and Pursell (1984). Third, to the extent that market size is increased by exporting possibilities, costs may fall as a result of economies of scale and an increased division of labour. Lastly, productivity in the economy as a whole may be increased as a result of the import of more productive inputs facilitated by the greater availability of foreign exchange. Effects such as these would go at least part of the way towards an explanation of South Korea's economic performance despite the export bias, the high levels of effective protection in selected areas, and the use of quantitative restrictions which, as we saw, presented difficulties for conventional trade theory. Findlay (1981) suggests as much when he argues that the reason why South Korea's export-oriented strategy has produced such successful results 'must be sought outside the conventional bounds of the standard model, in the murky but relevant waters of such concepts as X-efficiency and "learning-by-doing"' (p. 31).

However, it would probably be unwise to be too dogmatic about the relationship between economic performance and exports. To begin with, the requirements of the international market place may be too stringent, with the result that some firms may be unable to export and therefore gain from the beneficial effects discussed in the last paragraph. Related to this is the argument that export-oriented policies implicitly assume as a necessary precondition the attainment of a minimum threshold level of technological capabilities and that these can only be built up during a prior period of protected import substitution.[38] This is suggested by Nishimizu and Robinson (1983) who argue that:

In both Korea and Turkey, an import substitution phase was followed by a phase with significant export contributions to growth .... The observed phasing leads naturally to the hypothesis that a period of protected import substitution is useful—perhaps even necessary—to build a base from which a successful export drive, with associated positive total factor productivity growth, can be launched. (p. 32)

However, they note that the long-run benefits of such protection must outweigh the associated costs.[39]

It must be remembered, furthermore, that the *domestic* market plays a central role in the growth of countries like South Korea and Japan. Thus Krueger (1981) points out that 'the difference in growth rates [between "outward" and "inward" oriented economies] seem to be greater than can conceivably be accounted for by the exporting sector of the economy' (p. 4). In a footnote she notes that, 'Most observers of the international economy are astonished to learn that exports constitute only about 15 per cent of Japanese GNP, and that the share has been relatively constant since the early 1960s.'[40]

Further information on the importance of the domestic economy is provided in Nishimizu and Robinson (1983). In the case of Korea they estimate that while export expansion constituted an increasing source of growth of manufacturing demand (rising from 7 per cent in 1955–63 to 18 per cent in 1963–70 and 38 per cent in 1970–73), and import substitution a decreasing source (falling from 29 per cent to 0.2 per cent over the same period), domestic demand expansion comprised 64 per cent, 82 per cent and 63 per cent at the corresponding times. The figures for Japan are even more startling. Export expansion constituted 6 per cent, 10 per cent and 8 per cent of the growth of manufacturing demand for the years 1955–60, 1960–65 and 1965–70 while import substitution fell only slightly from—1.2 per cent to—0.1 per cent and—0.2 per cent over the same period. On the other hand domestic demand expansion comprised 95 per cent, 90 per cent and 92 per cent of the growth of manufacturing demand (p. 25, Table 4). This suggests that domestic influences, such as the degree of domestic competitive pressures (particularly in Japan) and other incentives, have been important in determining the growth of these two countries in addition to the advantages produced by their export sectors. Nishimizu and Robinson (1983) conclude from their study that 'import substitution regimes ... seem to be negatively correlated with total factor productivity change, whereas export expansion regimes are positively correlated with such change' (p. 25). However, the precise causal mechanisms remain to be analysed.

Moreover, technical progress, which as we saw Bell, Ross-Larson and Westphal (1983) argue is necessary for reductions in infant industry costs, occurs under both protected and more open regimes, although it has been suggested that the type of technical change may be different in each case. Thus Teitel (1984) concludes that:

it is not altogether clear how local technical activity depends one way or the other on the type and level of protection afforded to industrial activities. While ... technological research has been carried out under both circumstances—i.e. with and without protection—the nature of the technical change activity may be affected. That is, the technical change undertaken may tend to be more adaptive and less innovative in cases of high protection, and more cost-reducing in the case of relatively open economies. However, definite conclusions cannot yet be reached. (pp. 12-13)[41]

However, it must be kept in mind in examining this interim conclusion that economies such as those of South Korea are *both* open *and* protected.

TECHNOLOGY EXPORTS

The discussion thus far in this section has been largely concerned with the departure from free trade represented by infant protection, and with the technological processes associated with the maturation of infant industries. Another 'way in' to the examination of the importance of technological capabilities has been through the study of a particular category of exports, namely, exports of technology. In this sub-section we shall highlight some of the major issues and conclusions rather than attempt an exhaustive summary of the literature.

The growing body of research into technology exports from Third World countries was largely initiated by Katz (1978), Katz and Ablin (1979) and Lall (1979a). From both a 'rigid' dependency view and a neo-factor proportions theory of comparative advantage it seemed unlikely that Third World countries would be involved in the export of technology. However, perceptions have since changed with the accumulation of evidence of such exports. As Lall (1984a) notes, 'economists have taken technology exports to reveal the growing technological competence of industrializing countries and the most dynamic edge of their changing comparative advantage' (p. 1). But how large are these exports, which countries are the main exporters of technology and, most important for the present article, what precisely do technology exports reveal about a country's technological processes?

Owing to space limitations the question of the definition of technology exports and the available evidence on the relative performance of several of the more industrialised Third World countries are not discussed in detail here and the interested reader is referred to the relevant literature.[42] Some attention, however, will be given to the causal factors behind technology exports.

In a summary of the findings of a large on-going project Dahlman and Sercovitch (1984) note that in a large proportion of cases technology exporting firms enjoyed an international competitive advantage. They distinguish between four different types of advantage:

1. The first is a *cost advantage in providing basically the same type of process, product or service supplied by developed countries*. It is likely to be based primarily (but not exclusively) on lower wages, particularly those of skilled workers and engineers. Exports based on this type of advantage may be expected to go both to developed and to developing countries.

2. The second is an *advantage based on supplying an adapted or older process or product, or a technical service that is more appropriate* to the needs of the purchaser, because of some characteristics such as smaller scale, ease of operation, better knowledge of similar local environments, etc. Exports based on this type of advantage, which is rooted in technolgical experience in developing country conditions, may be expected to go to other developing countries.

3. The third is a *head start in experience which may be reflected in lower cost or greater appropriateness*. This advantage usually develops because of country-specific conditions such as the availability of natural resources and government promotion, whereby an acquired advantage in experience follows a natural advantage. Exports based on this type of advantage may go both to developed and developing countries.

4. The fourth is an *advantage based on having developed a technological breakthrough*. Exports based on this type of advantage may be expected to go both to developed and to developing countries. (pp. 29–30)

A similar distinction is made by Westphal and Rhee (1982). In assessing South Korea's 'revealed comparative advantage' in technology exports they distinguish between 'two alternative theories of comparative advantage', the 'neo-factor proportions' and 'neo-technological' theories.

The former assumes that technologies are universal and grounds a country's comparative advantage in its resource endowment, broadly conceived to include differentiated human capital. The latter assumes that technologies are idiosyncratic and thus emphasizes differences among technologies and their suitability for different economic environments. (pp. 55-7)

(For a related useful summary of recent theories of international trade and a discussion of the implications for the Third World, see Stewart (1982a)).

Not surprisingly, Dahlman and Sercovich (1984) note that most technology exports occur in the first two of their four categories and they conclude that 'most of the trade takes place in industries where the technology is more easily acquired because it has been around for a long time, and where it is relatively easy to keep up with the world frontier' (p. 20). In the case of South Korea Westphal and Rhee (1982) conclude that:

the preponderance of Korea's exports of technology appear to conform to the neo-factor proportions model. That is, the majority of Korea's technology exports reflect a comparative abundance of the skills involved primarily in establishing and secondarily in operating productive systems; only a minority reflect technological idiosyncracies. (p. 59)

Furthermore, 'the idiosyncratic technologies exported from India, Argentina, Mexico and Brazil reflect an intensity of technological effort and degree of innovativeness that are much greater than what is reflected in Korea's technology exports' (p. 59). In an examination of all the current evidence, Lall (1984a) concludes:

A survey of the country papers suggests that India leads in terms of both the diversity and complexity of the technologies in which technology export has taken place, followed at some distance by Argentina. Korea, Mexico and Brazil occupy the middle ground, and Taiwan and Hong Kong specialize in the narrowest range and least sophisticated technologies. (p. 12)

However, as Lall (1984a) notes, the papers surveyed do not 'aspire to answer fully the questions about what determines the acquisition of technological capability as revealed in technology exports' (p. 16). This brings us back to the question of the determinants of productivity and infant industry maturation and to the discussion earlier in the present survey of the sources of technical progress. Several points may be made. Dahlman and Sercovich (1984) conclude that 'some technological effort takes place regardless of the policy environment, such as the degree of inward versus outward trade orientation, or the emphasis on technological self-sufficiency' (p. 38). However,

the policy environment and characteristics such as the degree and type of competition do affect the direction of technological effort. For instance .... Indian firms appeared at least initially to devote a greater proportion of their effort than did firms in other less inwardly oriented countries to the substitution of imported raw materials and components; but Korean firms, which operated in a more outward oriented environment and faced greater price competition, appeared to devote technological effort more to cost reduction and to keeping up with new advances at the world frontier than on import substitution. (pp. 39–40)

Finally, they suggest that 'it is quite clear that a proper understanding of technological change cannot be exhausted within the limits of—or by extrapolating from—the single firm, or even a single industrial sector' (p. 40). A framework for thinking about this last point was suggested earlier in the present article in the discussion of the sources of technical progress. Furthermore, Lall (1984a) suggests that 'Large size of firm remains a positive influence on technology exports' (p. 15) and Dahlman and Sercovich (1984) note that:

a very clear feature is that in all of the countries surveyed most of the firms are locally-owned and controlled—even in Argentina, Brazil and Mexico, where there is the greatest presence of foreign investment. This suggests that as far as these firms are concerned, 'technology exports' do reflect increasing local technological capabilities. (p. 23)

But, if Lall is correct that 'India's technology exports ... embodies the greatest amount and spread of indigenous technological effort' (p. 16), then an explanation is clearly called for, especially since, as is well known, India's economic performance is not particularly impressive. In providing an explanation Lall (1984a) argues that:

The present evidence still supports [his] original hypothesis that the protection of domestic 'learning' (comprised of the protection of local manufacturing, particularly of capital goods, and of the protection of local technological effort by restricting access to imported technology) leads to a diverse and deep technological capability which spills over into technology exports.... Thus [in] India ... government intervention, almost unique in the newly industrialized country group for its inward-looking obsession on self-reliance, has been largely responsible for its accumulation of technical capabilities. (p. 17)

However, Lall suggests that India 'may also have generated a certain amount of socially wasteful technological effort which would have to be written off in a more open, competitive environment' and cautions that 'the costs of pushing technological effort too far leads to high cost, technological lags and various distortions which are very difficult to remove' (p. 18). None the less, his ultimate conclusion is: 'Some intervention is clearly needed to promote technological deepening. Such intervention may embrace both the production process (on classical infant industry grounds) ... and the technology-generation process (on protection of "learning" grounds)' (pp. 23–4).

SOME CONCLUSIONS AND POLICY IMPLICATIONS

Several conclusions may be drawn from the discussion in this section. To begin with, it would appear that the supposed link between free trade on the one hand and technical progress and productivity growth on the other has been considerably weakened. In the discussions of Krueger and Findlay it was noted that conventional trade theory does not provide any prediction of the effect of departures from free trade on the rate of growth. From an empirical point of view, instances were cited of the rapid attainment of international competitiveness under conditions of high rates of effective infant industry protection. While these appear to be exceptional, they support the conclusion that free trade is not a necessary condition for the achievement of international competitiveness (although this is not to deny that under some conditions free trade may assist such competitiveness). Furthermore, Lall has argued not only that relatively sophisticated technological capabilities have emerged in India under conditions of protection and promotion, but also that such conditions are necessary for the strengthening of these capabilities. On the 'other side' of the free trade position, Findlay's discussion of South Korea's export-biased industries showed that, although such biases were to be as strongly condemned from a conventional trade and welfare point of view as home-market biases, these industries had contributed substantially to this country's outstanding economic performance. The message thus appears to be that while technical progress is usually crucial for the achievement of increasing productivity and growth, free trade is not a necessary condition for the attainment of such progress.

One of the implications of this conclusion is that the significance of static comparative advantage as a 'guide post' to resource allocation is accordingly reduced. While short-run comparative costs will always have to enter into the calculations, the discussion of infant industries shows that an appreciation of the likely longer-run costs and benefits is necessary. By definition, infant industries do not enjoy a static comparative advantage. However, in view of the successful cases of infant industry protection, it would clearly be unsatisfactory automatically to exclude such industries for investment allocations on the grounds that they do not possess a static comparative advantage. As Bell, Ross-Larson and Westphal (1983) put it:

Several well-known empirical studies have investigated the costs of protection in various industrial sectors in developing economies. See, for example, Balassa and Associates (1971) and Little, Scitovsky, and Scott (1970); numerous similar studies have followed in the wake of these pioneering explorations. But almost all of these have been cross-sectional studies which only provide information about the distance (e.g. PQ in figure 1 [reproduced as Figure 1.2 above]) between ABC and FG at one time. Needed is information over time, not just at one time. Moreover, these studies are principally concerned with issues of allocative efficiency that are considered important from the perspective of the conventional paradigm of static comparative advantage. For several reasons, then, the studies throw little light on the issues being considered here. (p. 13)

However, as economists are painfully aware, the introduction into economic analysis of a time dimension that extends into the future creates substantial difficulties. Over time relevant factors change, and in ways that are not perfectly predictable. While institutionalised, routinised behaviour adds a degree of temporal continuity, it is important, as Nelson and Winter (1982) stress, 'to recognize that the flexibility of routinized behaviour is of limited scope and that a changing environment can force firms to risk their very survival on attempts to modify their routines' (p. 400). To make this abstract point more concrete, what 'guide posts' should an adviser to the Japanese government in the 1950s (that is, at time T_1 in Figure 1.2) have used in advising on the possible allocation of investment resources to the infant automobile industry? While, as we saw in the last section, MITI rejected the notion of short run comparative advantage, this principle was vigorously upheld by the President of the Bank of Japan. In the light of dilemmas such as these we shall examine in the following section some of the ways in which governments have intervened in the area of technology.

As Bell (1982) has noted:

project plans and appraisals depend critically on the assumed shape and average slope of the path ABC in [Figure 1.2] above. In many cases the assumed values appear to be rather arbitrarily determined (often resting, it seems, on general norms and 'experience' derived from industrialized economy situations). The apparently common experience of error in these assumptions does not seem to have led very often to systematic reviews of experience, or to the formulation of more appropriate norms. (p. 10)

As Nelson's (1981) survey of research on productivity growth clearly shows, we are a long way from being able to explain adequately inter-firm productivity differences. An example of this within the same industry in the same country is provided in Bell (1982: 32). Here it is noted that while in the Usiminas steel plant studied in Dahlman and Fonseca (1978) output per man in 1977 was 261 tons, the average for the industry as a whole was 113. While it is clearly ideal to be able to explain the divergence of average from best practice, and while further research into these questions should be high on the list of priorities, it seems, on the basis of present knowledge, that we have no alternative but to acknowledge that no reasonably firm answers yet exist. Accordingly, the policy dilemmas are, for the time being at least, unavoidable. While cost-benefit analysis will certainly assist in making explicit the assumptions that are made in project planning, and in examining the consequences of these assumptions, it is not capable, for the reasons discussed here, of overcoming all the problems of investment decision-making.

Related to this, is the question of the evaluation of different instruments of protection. As was seen above, the relative merits of subsidies, tariffs and quantitative restrictions have hitherto been discussed within the conceptual framework of static resource allocation. (The same framework has been used in the case of infant industries which is notable since, as we saw, the infant industry argument rests on inherently dynamic presuppositions.) From an empirical point of view the preference for quantitative restrictions and tariffs in, for example, South Korea and Japan, was noted, contradicting the conventional prescription in favour of subsidies. The successful economic performance of these countries, however, suggests that the time is ripe for a reconsideration, within a dynamic framework, of the costs and benefits of these instruments. While such an examination has not yet begun, it would seem that one of the central issues may well revolve around the question of uncertainty.

While, by definition, uncertainty does not exist under static assumptions, it is central in a world of dynamic change. As Corden (1980) has noted:

From the point of view of the protected firm, quotas can have the advantage of great certainty. Ideally, the potential domestic manufacturer would like assurance of a certain size market. If he believes that the size of the domestic market is not likely to change much, but that the principal source of uncertainty is the cost of competing imports, a quantitative quota on imports will certainly meet his needs.... This argument has obvious weight. It is particularly persuasive when, as is often the case, domestic production is subject to considerable economies of scale and there is little point in production being started at all unless there is assurance of a reasonable market. By contrast, there is uncertainty in the case of a tariff because it does not insulate the domestic price from foreign prices. (p. 82)

Accordingly, quotas can be particularly attractive to states like those of South Korea which has used a combination of carrots (protection and subsidies) and sticks (incentives contingent on export performance). While quotas add a considerable degree of certainty regarding profit expectations, subsidies (such as the generous subsidised credit extended by the South Korean state) have made the prospects even more attractive. The co-existence of these instruments may therefore appear to be far more reasonable than is apparent from a static welfare examination of their distortionary effects.

9 The State and Technical Change

Few would disagree that in all countries[43] the state plays a central role in shaping, stimulating and inhibiting various forms of technical change. Yet is it noteworthy that few comprehensive answers are available, within the context of specific countries, to crucial questions such as the following: why does the state intervene in technology matters in the way that it does, choosing some forms of intervention and rejecting others? How does the state make its decisions regarding intervention and what arguments are used in justification? How should the state decide on when, where and how to intervene? To take, for example, the literature on Japan,[44] a country which is at the forefront of discussions of technical change, it is noticeable that although a good deal is known about the forms of state intervention in the technology area, very little is known about how decisions were taken to intervene in these way, and about the interests and rationale involved in these decisions.[45] The same is true of the newly industrialised countries on which a good deal of the research on technology in the Third World has tended to concentrate.

Given the importance of state involvement in the field of technology, we shall examine in this section some of the forms of state intervention that are commonly found in some of the more industrialised Third World countries and Japan (the latter largely in the 1950s and 1960s) and then discuss briefly some of the theories of the state that have been used (implicitly or explicitly) in discussions of technology. No attempt will be made to evaluate the effectiveness of state intervention[46] and, because of the deficiencies in the literature just referred to, nothing will be said about why and how the particular state made decisions to intervene in the way it did.

STATE TECHNOLOGY POLICY

In this section we shall examine some common forms of state intervention in the technology area. To begin with, and closely related to the earlier discussion of market imperfections and the transfer of technology, many states have intervened in order to influence the *price* of imported technology.

A common form of intervention has been control exercised by the state over foreign technology agreements. In Japan, where this control was exerted by the powerful Ministry of International Trade and Industry (MITI), state efforts made a significant impact on the price of imported technology at least until 1968 when technology imports were liberalised to a greater extent than previously. Thus Peck and Tamura (1976) conclude that 'the overall effect of MITI intervention in the mid-1960s was to provide Japanese firms with technology on more favourable terms than they would have been able to obtain in the more open economies of the United States or Western Europe' (549–50).[47] However, MITI's interventions frequently went beyond scrutinisation of proposed foreign technology contracts.

The requirement of MITI approval served to reduce competition among Japanese firms, especially since there was sometimes informal designation by the MITI of a particular Japanese firm to negotiate with a specific foreign company. Beyond this, the MITI would delay its approval or make it conditional upon revisions that would lower rates. (ibid.: 548)[48]

MITI also attempted, wherever possible, to remove restrictive clauses from technology contracts such as those limiting exports although, with the relative strength of foreign technology suppliers in the 1960s, restrictions such as these remained common.

Similar controls have existed in South Korea where the acquisition of foreign technology has been subject to prior government scrutiny and approval. In the 1960s, as Amsden and Kim (1982) point out, the criteria used in appraising technology contracts included the following: '(1) royalties should not exceed 3%; (2) contract periods should not exceed 5 years; (3) export restriction clauses should not be included' (p. 33). Before the mid-1970s there was relatively little licensing in South Korea. However, with the initiation of the heavy industrialisation programme in 1973 controls were to some extent liberalised leading to an increase in both the number of contractual agreements and royalty payments. Similar controls have been instituted in other countries (see, for example, Dahlman (1982) on Brazil and Lall (1984b) on India).

Related to state attempts to reduce the price of imported technology have been attempts to influence the *form* of such imports. The form of technology import may to some extent influence the price but it may also have a bearing on the net social benefit of the imported technology. Thus, for example, many governments have intervened, where this has been deemed to be feasible, to limit the control of foreign capital, particularly wholly-owned direct foreign investment. An implicit reason for such intervention (although the precise rationale is seldom made explicit by governments) is the assumption that other forms of technology import will often provide greater benefit. In the case of Brazil, for example, Dahlman (1982) refers to the

specific measures adopted by the government to limit the increase in foreign participation in the economy. They have included giving local firms preference in purchase by state owned companies, providing equity capital through the subsidiaries of the National Development Bank (BNDE) to create joint ventures and strengthen local firms, and prohibiting foreign firms from acquiring Brazilian companies which the government considers leaders in priority fields. (p. 12)

In Japan efforts to reduce foreign control over all aspects of technology transfer were facilitated by the enactment of the Foreign Capital Law (Gaishi Hō, number 163 of 10 May, 1950). Johnson (1982) notes that this law 'established a Foreign Investment Committee and stipulated that foreign investors wanting to license technology, acquire stock, share patents, or enter into any kind of contract that provided them with assets in Japan had first to be licensed (kyoka) by the Committee' (p. 217). Peck and Tamura (1976) suggest that while the official rationale for such controls lay in concern for the balance of payments situation and the possibility of disruption to the small-business sector, 'More important than any stated rationale for controls is their impact on the price of technology, the composition of the imported technology, and the industrial structure–all areas in which the evidence suggests that government controls did make a difference' (p. 546). They note that 'Direct investment was successively liberalized by Japan beginning in 1967' although they point out (in 1976) that 'the extent to which the liberalization in fact means full freedom for direct investment is a matter of debate' (p. 551).

Similarly, in South Korea, Amsden and Kim (1982) point out that the Foreign Capital Promotion Law, passed first in 1960, regulates both foreign direct investment and the acquisitions of foreign technology. South Korea, they note, 'has been one of the few LDCs with very restrictive regulations on foreign investment and technology transfer' (p. 27). While this law also provided incentives for foreign investment, the latter remained at low levels until 1965 when diplomatic relations with Japan were re-established. In 1973 a major policy change took place motivated by the 'fear that an unlimited inflow of foreign investment might have adverse effects on the economy' (ibid.). In this year three criteria were established in connection with direct foreign investment.

First, project eligibility criteria disallowed projects that might compete with domestic firms in either the domestic or international markets, or that might disrupt domestic demand and supply of raw materials and intermediate goods. Second, foreign ownership criteria limited foreign participation to 50% unless projects were entirely export-oriented or technology-intensive and led to important export or import-substitution production. Third, investment scale criteria set (the amount for) minimum investment. (pp. 28–9)

In 1980, however, the restrictions on foreign investment were liberalised and foreign firms came to play an important role in sectors such as electronics, oil refining and fertilisers (ibid.: 31).

In addition to attempting to influence the price of foreign technology and the form in which technology is imported, the state has also used technology policy to effect changes in the *structure* of industry. An example of this is Japan where in 1950 the MITI announced a list of 33 'desired technologies' which would be given priority in the approval of technology agreements. Most of the technologies were in the area of heavy industry, only three technologies relating to consumer goods. In 1959 additions were made to the list for 'electronic and jet aircraft items and for techniques making processes continuous, more efficient, or automated in any industry' (Peck and Tamura, 1976: 552). While agreement was also granted for technologies not on the MITI's list, 'controls apparently did suppress the demand for foreign technology' (ibid.). In much the same way as we saw earlier that the selective imposition of quotas and tariffs influenced industrial structure in South Korea by encouraging infant industries, Peck and Tamura suggest that the control of access to foreign technology influenced the structure of industry in Japan. 'Access to imported technology was a major source of profit, and to deny such access to some industries served to tilt the pattern of investment and output toward what were regarded as basic industries' (p. 553). However, approval of a technology agreement was 'conditional upon its meeting the MITI's interests, first in the construction of plants of efficient scale and second, in avoiding excess capacity and the ensuing price competition' (ibid.). While MITI at times attempted to bring new firms into industries this was 'never at the expense of unused capacity or excessive competition' (ibid.).

Measures designed to influence industrial structure while at the same time building up *local technological capabilities* have included the placing of restrictions on the import of technology. Once example of such measures is the attempt that has been made in a number of countries to encourage the development of a local capital goods sector. In some of these countries the import of embodied technology has been prohibited in the event of the availability of national 'similars'. In Brazil, for example, according to the Law of National Similars, passed originally in 1966, restrictions have been placed on the import of capital goods (see Tyler, 1981). Furthermore, as Dahlman (1982) points out, investment incentive schemes favoured the purchase of locally produced capital goods and the government 'sought to use purchases by state owned enterprises to stimulate the domestic capital goods industry' (p. 14). Furthermore, 'government policy has favoured the development of the locally-owned capital goods industry' (p. 16). Similarly, in India, Lall (1984b) notes that 'the protection given to indigenous manufacturers has resulted in a broad-based, diverse and complex capital goods sector (p. 232).

In South Korea, Amsden and Kim (1982) point out that while 'Easy access to imported capital goods was a cornerstone of the government's strategy to initiate industrialization on the basis of light industries oriented towards exports', the situation changed with the adoption of the heavy industrialisation programme (p. 53). They note that 'the controversial measure to encourage heavy industry consists of the imposition of quantitative controls on competing imports ("similars") immediately upon the initiation of domestic production ... Much use appears to be made of this provision in recent years' (pp. 56–7). Furthermore, tariff exemptions on imported machinery and equipment are 'subject to the conditions that the imported capital goods be essential to the manufacturing process, embody the latest technology, and not be domestically produced' (p. 55). In addition, medium-and-long-term credit has been provided for the production or purchase of locally-produced machinery. 'These funds are supposed to finance 70–80% of buyers' outlays on locally produced capital goods' (ibid.).

In their social cost-benefit analysis of the choice between imported and locally made looms for cotton textile weaving in South Korea, Rhee and Westphal (1977) concluded that 'the policies encouraging the use of imported technology simultaneously discriminate against domestic textile machinery manufacturers, thus inappropriately retarding the development of the domestic engineering industry' (p. 235). To the extent that the measures to encourage the local capital goods sector, introduced after the Rhee and Westphal study was undertaken, correct such discrimination, net social benefits will clearly be increased. However, it is necessary to add, going back to the discussion of infant industries, that such calculations are usually not made in a rigorous way prior to the decision to selectively encourage parts of the industrial sector. In the case of Taiwan, Westphal (1978a) notes that:

Discussions with the staff of the Industrial Development Board disclosed that the criteria underlying the selection of industries for fixed investment incentives include only technical feasibility and marketing potential, while it is also evident that attention is paid to economies of scale .... Benefit-cost analysis is not employed as a discriminant .... It is apparently felt that economic analysis is best conducted by potential sponsors, who are more likely to possess or develop information at the requisite level of detail.[49]

Other state interventions to encourage local technological capabilities include the provision of finance to encourage the development of human science and technology skills, to encourage the adaptation and improvement of foreign technology and to stimulate other forms of local R & D. In many instances the state has also directly made decisions regarding technology through the state ownership and control of technology-using and generating firms and institutions. In Brazil, for example, as Baranson (1981) points out, 'sixteen of Brazil's twenty largest firms were operated by the state, which owned eighty-six percent of the total assets involved' (p. 19).

The discussion of state intervention in the area of technology in this section has been illustrative rather than exhaustive. In the following section a few observations will be made about the degree of influence wielded over the private sector by the state.

THE STATE AND THE PRIVATE SECTOR

An important phenomenon that has been widely referred to in the literature, but which remains poorly understood, relates to the degree of influence exerted by some states over economic decision-making, including decisions relating to technology. In the case of Japan, for example, Rosovsky (1972) has stated:

In considering the sweep of Japanese economic history, I am struck by the notion that government–business relations were, from the local point of view, well arranged. Japan retained some advantages of capitalism (i.e. efficient producers), while reaping certain benefits of socialism (i.e. considerable public control of the economic effort and direction) (p. 249).

Certainly the student of the MITI's activity (see in particular the informative book by Johnson (1982)) is struck by the considerable degree of influence exerted by this branch of the state. That this influence has been used in a way that is generally beneficial is suggested by Johnson's characterisation of the 'developmental state' in Japan. Jones and Sakong (1980) refer similarly to the 'strong state' in South Korea, although this appropriately relates more to the post-Syngman Rhee period. Sen (1983) suggests:

The government played a major part in fostering economic growth in South Korea, and as has been argued, no state outside the socialist bloc ever came anywhere near this measure of control over the economy's investible resources. Indeed ... the South Korean government had control over two-thirds of the investible resources in the country in the period of its rapid acceleration of growth. This governmental power was firmly used to guide investment in chosen directions through differential interest rates and credit availabilities .... Even Korean export expansion was founded on building an industrial base through severe import controls before export promotion was promoted and even now the import of many items is restricted or prohibited. (p. 13)

With reference to the import of technology Enos (1982) has suggested that the South Korean state has intervened, in general, in order to secure the greatest national benefit:

... the Korean Government deliberately and consistently imports industrial technology of the most modern type under terms that assure that equipment will be operated by its own citizens to the fullest extent, and that the goods which are produced will be made available, at reasonable prices and steady rates, to domestic manufacturers and distributors. (p. 75)

However, 'such matters do not stand at the top of the list of priorities of other developing countries' (ibid.). In these countries the personal return (in financial and prestige terms) of bureaucrats is often of prime importance (p. 77). 'Once contracts have been signed, concern over the absorption of that technology into the importing country seems often to lapse, at least on the part of those who made the decision to adopt it' (ibid.).

Clearly, the phenomenon of a state which is 'strong' in terms both of its degree of influence *vis-à-vis* the private sector, and the beneficial effects of its policies,[50] is important in any discussion of economic policy in general and technology policy in particular. However, it will be noted, from the quotations above as well as from the original sources, that comments on the 'strong state' have been primarily of a descriptive kind. An important task remains to explain the emergence of such a state, the difference in perspective and approach between this state and private capital, and the consequences of all this for economic performance.

THEORIES OF THE STATE

Much of the literature dealing with state intervention in the area of technology in the Third World implicitly incorporates a model of the 'state as rational subject'. According to this implicit model, the state's objective is to maximise the social welfare of the nation as a whole and the state should rationally choose appropriate policies in order to achieve this objective. Welfare economics, and in particular the world of second-best, is regarded as *the* guide to the rational state's economic policy.[51] As in other areas of economic policy, a necessary condition for state intervention in the field of technology is that the resulting social benefits must exceed the social costs.

However, quite apart from the question of the theoretical adequacy of the assumptions of welfare economics,[52] this view of the state and of the process of decision-making in the area of technology faces a number of serious problems. To begin with, as we have seen, the injunction that social benefit must exceed social cost may offer very little assistance in (*ex ante*) decision-making. Under conditions of uncertainty, and the uncertainty will usually be great given the relatively long-time horizons associated with technology decisions, social costs and benefits cannot be estimated with a sufficient degree of accuracy.[53] For present purposes the main implication is that the possibility of an unambiguously 'rational' state policy breaks down. We saw earlier, for example, that what seemed to be 'rational' from MITI's point of view in Japan was 'irrational' from the perspective of the President of the Bank of Japan.[54] With no unambiguous 'guide' to show the way, the door is opened to differences and disputes regarding desirable courses of policy intervention based on differing interests, perspectives and degrees of political power. Furthermore, the present discussion implies that this state of affairs will be the rule rather than the exception. Accordingly, in understanding the 'making of technology policy' as a prelude to examining the effects of such policy, it will be necessary to analyse these interests, perspectives, and political power factors. (For a most illuminating analysis of the kind implied here see Dore's (1983) discussion of the Next Generation Base Technologies Development Programme which involved selection in Japan of technologies for development for the 1990s.) Such an analysis would enable us to understand why technology policy, and technical progress itself, evolves in the way that it does in any particular country at any time. The problem with the theory of the 'state as a rational subject' is that it usually remains implicit, with the result that questions such as those discussed here are neither posed, nor answered.

This can present problems in all areas of economic policy as has emerged, to take an example, in some of the discussions of South Korean policy. Thus Krueger (1981) notes that:

> the political–economic interactions in policy making are little understood ... the decision to undertake import-substitution policies is obviously not completely independent of the underlying economic and political situation ... whether policy makers choose import substitution because they have different objectives from the ones adopting export promotion, whether they are constrained politically to adopt import-substitution policies, despite the fact that they know better, or whether import-substitution policies of the sort described have been adopted out of a lack of understanding of the economic process is an important question. (pp. 23–4)

Lying as they do outside the implicit model of the state, questions like these are all too seldom posed. However, as the quotation from Krueger implies, much of the conventional discussion of economic policy implicitly assumes that the state is an entity which exists 'outside' of society. The objective of economic policy analysis is to supply the autonomous state with a rational set of guidelines. But, as Krueger notes, economic policy is not 'completely independent' of the underlying economic and political circumstances.

This, however, raises further difficult questions. If state decisions and interventions are to some extent determined by 'underlying social and economic processes' in the society, how are these processes to be examined and how is their influence on state policy to be assessed? Indeed, to take this one step further, can the state be understood as an entity distinct from, and influenced by, political and economic processes that are external to it, or is it better to see the state as an integral part of these processes? At this point in the discussion many economists will have the uncomfortable feeling that we are wandering too far afield into the territories of neighbouring disciplines where we lack the necessary conceptual knowledge.

Better that we return to the familiar home ground. However, as Krueger implies, this may be short-sighted precisely because we may miss many of the important determining influences on economic policy. Furthermore, as we have suggested, an understanding of these influences is particularly important since under the conditions of uncertainty that usually apply, there will be no single, rational choice and accordingly social and political processes will come to exert an important influence on economic policy-making.

A second view often associated with different (and at times contradictory) Marxist theories of the state, has tended to approach the state through an analysis of the major social forces existing in the society. According to this view the state is not an 'independent' force in society. Rather its interventions are best seen as a reflection of the economic and political interests existing within the society. In the Third World technology context this view (or something like it) has been used, for example, in discussions of whether technology policy is influenced more by 'international' or 'national' interests. These discussions imply a divergence in interest between these two groups and also, possibly, differing assumptions regarding the presumed outcome of alternative directions in technology policy. The main strength of this approach, in contrast to the previous one, is that no assumption is made regarding rationality and certainty, and an unequal distribution of political power, which can shift over time, is allowed for. However, problems arise from the inherent difficulty of establishing which social groups are dominant in terms of their influence over state policy (for example, international or national elements, agricultural or industrial, feudal or capitalist) and of defining what constitute their long-term interests. Elster (1983) is no doubt correct when he suggests that many such theories have put forward functionalist arguments that are teleological. These arguments are unacceptable as explanations since they fail to posit a 'feedback mechanism' that will ensure that the state acts in some ways rather than others.[55]

However, whether or not an acceptable theory of state intervention exists, or could be constructed, the fact remains that we have no answers to the central questions posed at the beginning of this section. This is a problem since it is obviously important to have an understanding of why particular policies were followed rather than others, under conditions where there are few 'obviously correct' solutions (though there may be more that are obviously incorrect). To return to the Japanese example, it would be extremely interesting to establish how in the post-Second World War period, having rejected the determining principle of static comparative advantage, decisions were made to specialise in particular areas and to invest in technological capabilities of different levels. An examination of this question would raise a large number of important issues including that of the relationship between, on the one hand, the various, and at times contradictory, centres of influence within the state, and on the other, the different centres of influence within the private sector.

10 Conclusion

Part I has provided an interpretive survey of many of the issues that have appeared since the latter 1970s in the area of technology in the Third World. Perhaps the most important point to emerge from the discussion is that, while central questions remain to be clarified, as pointed out in various places in the survey, a start has certainly been made in unravelling the complex factors that together shape the process of technical change. It is true that we still lack a rigorous theory of technical change and as a result are unable to explain inter-firm, inter-country and inter-temporal differences in technical change and productivity. But, as this survey has hopefully illustrated, there are areas where the mist has begun to lift a little, even though the full view is not yet entirely clear.

This conclusion has depressing as well as more optimistic undertones. It is depressing when we realise, looking back, that although Adam Smith began the *Wealth of Nations* with an examination of the causes of technical change and productivity increases, we are today unable to report an enormous amount of progress. This in itself is worthy of further examination. From the time of the classical economists, with the notable exception of Schumpeter, mainstream economics has been relatively little concerned with the causes (as opposed to the consequences) of technical change. From the marginal revolution in the latter nineteenth century, mainstream economics has been far more concerned with market phenomena than with the activities involved in production. The prices of both pins and the inputs required for their manufacture have been of more interest than the factors influencing the ways in which pins are produced. Keynes was also not particularly concerned with technical change. In Keynes' world of the 1930s the major problem appeared to be that of marrying the workers standing in the dole queues with the technically and economically efficient machinery lying idle in the factories. In such a world the production of better machinery was hardly an issue. Neither mainstream microeconomics, nor mainstream macroeconomics, has yet found a home for the causes of technical change. This is paradoxical, of course, since technical change and productivity lie at the heart of costs, competitiveness, and economic growth.

The conclusion in the first paragraph, however, also has its optimistic side since it has been claimed that some progress has been made in understanding the factors that shape technical change. This too requires further examination. What factors account for the progress that has been made?

In large part, it may be suggested, the progress is due to the changes that have occurred in the conceptualisation of technical change. Increasingly attempts are being made to understand what happens between the moment of purchase of factor inputs at prevailing factor prices and the moment when the resulting output becomes available for sale. In other words, the transformation process itself, whereby inputs are converted into outputs, and changes in this process, are coming under scrutiny. In examining the transformation process it is being increasingly realised that firms are far more than entities which maximise profits on the basis of the array of factor and product prices and the 'given' technology. Rather, they are complex social organisations linked to the outside world through their activities of buying, producing and selling. In understanding the causes of technical change it is necessary to examine influences both internal and external to the firm. Those influences are numerous and interact in a complex way and market price is only one of the mediums through which the influence is exerted. By conceptualising the 'firm' and its interaction with its 'environment' in a different way, the door has been opened to a more fruitful examination of the causes of technical change.

Finally, in view of the soul-searching that is currently in vogue among development economists (see, for example, Hirschman (1982) and W.A. Lewis's Presidential Address to the American Economic Association (1984)), it might be worth adding a few words on the contribution of development economics when viewed from the vantage-point of the study of technology in the Third World.

Comment here will be restricted to two points. The first is that in the area of the study of technology there is an increasing convergence of perspective between those working, on both industrialised and Third World countries, under what has been referred to in this survey as a neo-Schumpeterian banner. It must be added, however, that this perspective has found more fertile ground amongst development economists than amongst economists working on industrialised countries. In their pragmatic and eclectic way, putting a higher priority on coming to grips with real world problems than on formal elegance, development economists have more readily adopted a perspective that, while not yet welded into a rigorous theoretical paradigm, nevertheless offers considerable scope for understanding the determinants of technical change.

At first glance, this convergence seems strange in view of the huge technology-gap that exists between the highly industrialised and all Third World countries. A major theme in post-war development economics has been the need for a different mode of analysis for Third World countries in view of the special conditions existing in these countries. Surely a similar argument applies in the case of the study of technology? A major point to emerge in studies of technology, however, negates this argument. This is the realisation that over time incremental technical change is usually of greater significance than radical frontier-shifting change. Accordingly, the story of technical change in the highly industrialised countries is by no means entirely one of breakthroughs by highly trained scientists and engineers. While such events certainly occur in these industrialised countries rather than in Third World countries, far more typical, and more significant in the longer run, are incremental changes of the kind which appear in all countries. Although in terms of consequences the technical changes might on the whole be much greater in the industrialised countries than in the Third World, in terms of causes, and more importantly in terms of the approach needed to analyse such changes, the situation may not be too different.

The second comment, following on from the first, is that it might not be immodest to suggest that development economists working on technical change in the Third World are contributing to a body of knowledge that will be crucial in understanding technical change in the industrialised countries. The Japanese example is important since here international diffusion of technology and incremental technical change, central issues for the development economist working on technology, made important contributions to this country's ultimate achievement of international competitiveness. It might, furthermore, be suggested that many development economists, in view of the pragmatic nature of their discipline, might be better placed than many of their professional colleagues working on industrialised countries to adopt and adapt the new paradigms that will have to emerge in the quest to understand better the causes of technical change. As emphasised in this survey, the past paradigms have run their course and the phenomenon of technical change remains to be fully understood.

PART II
Directions for Future Research

11 Some Research Priorities

INTRODUCTION

The aim of this chapter is to discuss some of the research implications that follow from the survey contained in Chapter 1.

Two preliminary points must be made. The suggestions for research made in this chapter deal largely with the development of *new* ways of conceptualising economic change and related technological development. However, this is not to argue that these represent the only way forward. There may well be others that are not considered here. Furthermore, there are still many issues that remain to be more thoroughly explored even though they fall under the heading of 'older' ways of conceptualising technical change. At many points in the survey, it is either explicitly or implicitly clear where the present writer feels that further research is desirable. No attempt, however, is made here to elaborate on these research suggestions. Secondly, in pointing to possible directions for future research, only the general outlines of a research programme are considered. The detailed hypotheses, research questions and arguments still remain to be elaborated.

THE NEED FOR NEW DIRECTIONS

One of the main implications to emerge from the survey in

115

Part I relates to the shortcomings of the conceptual approaches that tended to dominate the present area of research until the late 1970s. In this connection particular attention was paid to neoclassical economics and dependency theory. However, care must be taken not to negate totally the contributions made by these schools of thought. In the case of neoclassical economics, for example, the survey also highlighted the importance of such contributions as: social cost-benefit analysis; in the area of trade theory, concepts such as the effective rates of protection and subsidy, the domestic resource cost of foreign exchange and the analysis of the effects of tariffs and subsidies; the measurement of total factor productivity, etc.

These contributions have been primarily concerned with the efficient allocation of *given* resources. Such contributions have an obvious appeal since they seem to offer a way of improving efficiency through a reallocation of resources. And such questions must be high on the priority-list of governments in less developed countries. For example, is it efficient to put scarce and therefore relatively costly resources into the production of, say, motor cars, steel or machine-tools in a middle-income country rather than allocating these same resources to other purposes? Is it better to produce certain kinds of machines domestically, or allocate the same resources to the export sector in order subsequently to import the machines that are required? The importance of questions such as these can hardly be denied. However, as significant as these kinds of questions are, the substantive issue is how to *answer* them.

It is here that serious analytical problems begin to emerge. In a world in which it is reasonable to assume that resources, technology, and productivity either remain constant or change in predictable ways, neoclassical economics is well equipped to answer the sorts of question that have just been posed. However, this is essentially a *timeless* world devoid of novelty and surprise. In short, it is not the world in which we live. As Bergson (1963) put it: 'The further we penetrate the analysis of the nature of time, the more we understand that duration signifies invention, creation of forms and the continual elaboration of what is absolutely new.' In such a world economic change is a constant process of becoming and involves the continual injection of the new and the unexpected. Hence the issues of changing knowledge (including technological knowledge) and uncertainty are central. However, as a result of its starting assumptions, both implicit and explicit, neoclassical economics is severely limited in its ability to deal adequately with such a world.

The usefulness of neoclassical economics in analysing problems of economic development is further restricted by the inadequate conceptualisation of the firm in this body of thought. McNulty (1984) has noted in an important article that:

economics emerged from the hands of Adam Smith as an analytical blend of firm and market forces. But it was not a balanced blend. The analytical core of his work was in the operations of the pricing system, and this became, with the subsequent development of economics, increasingly the focus of theory. This single-minded focus on the market was accompanied and made possible, it is important to note, only as the nature and focus of economics itself shifted, away from Smith's primary emphasis on economic growth and development, toward the study of allocation and distribution .... As distribution or allocation came increasingly to the forefront of economic analysis, production, in the sense of the physical or qualitative transformation of resources, which had been the initial analytical focus of the *Wealth Of Nations*, was pushed increasingly into the background, and with it, the role of the firm – the organisation through which that transformation had been effected. This was accompnaied, as economics developed and aspired to scientific status, by a growing role for the concept of market competition. (p. 239)

Neoclassical economics lacks a convincing theory of production and, correspondingly, an adequate theory of technical change. In neoclassical economics the process of production tends to be reduced, via the concept of the production possibility set which is 'given' to all firms and known by them with certainty and the assumption of profit-maximisation, to a series of decisions based on market prices.

Market prices therefore become the driving force in the system while the sphere of production becomes devoid of content. This further limits the usefulness of neoclassical economics in the quest to analyse processes of economic development and suggests that new conceptualisations are required in order to deal more satisfactorily with the process of production.

Although for different reasons, dependency theory–at least in its rigid form–has similarly been unable to deal with the process of technical and productivity change in less developed countries. A body of thought which has been concerned to emphasise the constraints on the process of growth in these countries has not proved to be suited to the analysis of the process of technical and productivity change. Nevertheless, important constraints certainly do confront less developed countries, and dependency theory has served to improve understanding of the ways in which some of these constraints operate.

Accordingly, while both neoclassical economics, with its stress on the efficient allocation of given resources and market phenomena, and dependency theory, with its analysis of the constraints on accumulation in less developed countries, have made their contribution, they have serious shortcomings when applied to a world of economic and technical change.

In the survey of the first Part of this book, it is pointed out that for a number of related reasons neoclassical economics and dependency theory, hitherto the two dominant paradigms in this field of study, began to lose their influence in the latter half of the 1970s. One manifestation of this was the increasing number of studies on the process of technical change in less developed countries and the consequences of this change. While these studies revealed that it was primarily incremental technical change that occurred, they also showed that the cumulative effects of such change could be substantial. Some of the studies done in the newly industrialised countries in Latin America and Asia (discussed at length in the survey) demonstrated that foreign technology could be sucessfully mastered, adapted to local circumstances and, in a few instances, substantially improved upon. In these cases it was suggested that a different 'trajectory' of technological development had occurred compared with that in the more highly industrialised countries. In some instances this evolutionary process had resulted in products and processes that were significantly different from those produced in richer countries, and this difference was reflected in South–South flows of trade and investment.

From the point of view of the conceptual concerns of the present chapter, however, these studies are of interest less as a result of their empirical findings (important though these are), but more because of their theoretical implications. The major implication of these studies was that if the process of economic change in less developed countries is to be understood, an analysis of technical change is essential. Furthermore, if technical change is to be understood it is necessary to examine the process of change at the level of the firm while analysing the influences of macroscopic factors, including international circumstances. This in turn raised further difficulties as a result of the absence of an appropriate conceptual framework with which to tackle these issues. As noted, neither neo-classical economics nor dependency theory supplied the requisite tools. This presented the authors of the studies with a problem. While they drew heavily on what was referred to in the survey as the neo-Schumpeterian literature that was beginning to emerge in the highly industrialised countries (specific mention was made of the contributions of writers such as Rosenberg and Nelson and Winter), this literature provided many helpful suggestions and insights rather than a fully developed set of conceptual tools. As a result, the studies on technical change in less developed countries tended to be primarily empirical. The best of these studies, however, had important consequences. To begin with, they changed fundamentally the dominant image of these countries. While hitherto less developed countries were seen as technologically dormant (by dependency theory), or as able to specialise only in unskilled labour-intensive and technology-unintensive commodities (by the neoclassical theory of comparative advantage), now these same countries tended to be seen as actively involved in the process of economic change. The second consequence of these studies, following on from the first, was that they made it clear that a fundamental reconceptualisation of the nature of the firm was necessary. No longer was it adequate to see firms as decision-making centres which maximise profits on the basis of demand and supply conditions on input and output markets and a technological knowledge set somehow 'given' to all participants. This conceptualisation, it became increasingly clear, was more of a hindrance than a help in the attempt to understand the process of production and related technological development in less developed countries. Rather, new ways of viewing the firm had to be developed taking account of the specific conditions that existed in these countries.

By clarifying these issues (in most cases implicitly) these studies have had a significant impact. In turn, they suggest that the time is now ripe for further attention to be paid to the task of developing more appropriate conceptual tools. By providing a relatively firm base of empirical information (but one that needs to be extended) these studies have also performed the useful function of 'guiding' the conceptual work that is necessary. The *starting*-point for theorising in this area, therefore, is not an abstract set of simplifying assumptions but rather empirical processes of economic and technical change. While abstraction is always an essential part of the process of theorising, the empirical studies referred to serve as a constant reminder of what is to be explained and therefore as an 'anchor' for the conceptual work that is needed.

To the extent that the above serves as an adequate summary of the current state of affairs in this field of study the next question that must be addressed relates to the priorities for research in the immediate future. This question is tackled in the following section.

SOME DIRECTIONS FOR FUTURE RESEARCH

In proposing some directions for future research a number of preliminary points must be kept in mind. To begin with, it must be reiterated that we are still in a pre-paradigmatic stage with regard to the conceptualisation of the process of technical change in less developed countries. A rigorous proposal for research, posing problems and suggesting directions for solutions, has not yet emerged. In such a situation it is probably wise to opt for a plurality of approaches in the hope that greater clarity will emerge from the competing of alternative approaches than from the pursuance of single directions. Accordingly, the present proposals for future research must be seen as one set of suggestions among a variety of possibilities.

Secondly, it is suggested that whatever approaches are to be pursued it is important that both theoretical and empirical work to be undertaken concurrently. The reason is that, while we lack appropriate conceptual tools of analysis, we also lack the empirical (including historical) information on which to base attempts at theorising. For the paradigmatic reasons considered in the last section, there is a dearth of good empirical studies on the processes of change in production in less developed countries. The interplay between theoretical and empirical work will accordingly be mutually advantageous.

In the remainder of this section an attempt will be made to outline some of the areas in which both theoretical and empirical work is needed. In examining the elements of a new conceptualisation it will be useful to highlight both the notions that need to be transcended as well as the new perspectives that must be developed. The following six areas are identified for further research: reconceptualising the firm; the firm and its environment: a microscopic/macroscopic analysis; changes in technological knowledge; change in organisations and resistance to change; diffusion and selection processes; the state. Rather than providing a detailed analysis of these areas here, attention is confined to a consideration of some of the main features of such an analysis.

ELEMENTS OF A NEW CONCEPTUALISATION OF TECHNICAL CHANGE

(a). Reconceptualising the firm

In reconceptualising the firm we need to move away from the view which reduces the activities of the firm to a series of profit-maximising calculations on the basis of given technology and market conditions towards an alternative view which sees firms as interacting 'social organisms'.

The internal structures of firms as well as their mode of operating have an important bearing on the processes of production which they coordinate. In analysing these structures and operations a useful link may be made with the work of organisation theorists. Here it is possible only to point to a few of the factors which might be taken into account in such analyses.

The work of Williamson (1975) in this area is a useful starting-point. In the attempt to correct the imbalance noted in the quotation above from McNulty (1984), Williamson stressed the fundamental differences between the operations of markets and the operations of hierarchies within firms. While the former involve transactions between relatively autonomous (though possibly dependent in various degrees) parties, the latter involve hierarchically structured, superior–subordinate relationships. One of Williamson's concerns has been to emphasise that in some circumstances markets and hierarchies constitute alternative forms of organisation (for example, components can be produced in-house or alternatively bought from a subcontractor) and that a choice therefore exists between them. An analysis of transactions costs, Williamson argues, will determine how this choice is made. While Williamson's work has generated a good deal of debate that will not be considered here, the importance of his contribution for present purposes is that it serves to emphasise the duality that exists in capitalist societies–namely, the coexistence of markets and hierarchies, and the need to take both into account in the analysis of economic change. Furthermore, it stresses the importance of hierarchical forms of organisation within firms. In turn, this line of thinking raises many other issues which have not yet been raised in the context of less developed countries. More specifically, it highlights the fact that the process of production, including the process of technical change, takes place within the context of a set of hierarchically structured relationships which influence it. To be more accurate, the processes of production and technical change are themselves structured by the hierarchical relationships which exist in the firm. The analysis of technical change therefore also requires an analysis of hierarchy.

This in turn raises further issues. For example, by whom, how and on what basis are decisions made regarding technical change? What sorts of consideration are taken into account in opting for one or other course of action? How are these decisions implemented within the set of hierarchically structured relationships? How are conflicts regarding desirable directions of technical change resolved? By posing and attempting to answer questions such as these it becomes apparent that decisions regarding technology, and therefore the technological operations of firms, are far more complex than is usually allowed for in the economics literature. An understanding of the determinants of technical change may therefore have a good deal to gain from a more careful study of organisations and their modes of operation and change.

A further area that must feature prominently in any reconceptualisation of the firm relates to the firm's stock of knowledge. While technological knowledge is conventionally considered in economics to be either 'given' to all firms or purchased as an 'input' by them in a way analogous to the purchase of other inputs, this is a simplification that might conceal more than it reveals. Here too a more careful study is needed of questions such as the following: How do firms acquire the various components of their stock of technological knowledge, distinguishing between the various internal and external sources of acquisition? How is this knowledge assimilated by, and stored in, the firm? What sorts of process are involved in the selection and structuring of technological knowledge?

Regarding the last point, important work has been done applying the concept of paradigm developed by Kuhn to the field of technology. Technological paradigms are seen as forming the basis according to which technological knowledge is selected, structured and further developed. The selection and structuring of such knowledge can have important consequences. For example, in an important study of Japanese manufacturing techniques Schonberger (1982) has shown that basic questions relating to the coordination of production have been answered in a highly selective way. Standard mass-production practices in the United States have until recently placed emphasis on the role of buffer stocks to absorb shocks resulting from disruptions in supplies. Furthermore, quality has tended to be controlled through the activities of a functionally specialised production department which has carried out routine statistical checks on quality to ensure that acceptable defect rates are achieved. However, in Japan, a fundamentally different technological paradigm emerged under the conditions prevailing in the early post-Second World War period when the low quality of Japanese manufactured products, together with the need to generate foreign exchange through exports, combined to encourage the search for new approaches to reduce costs and increase quality. With the initial assistance of a number of American authorities on production techniques in the 1950s, Japanese manufacturers in the discrete products industries perfected the so-called 'just in time' system in which components are produced in-house and purchased from subcontractors to be delivered just in time to be assembled, thus avoiding the necessity for buffer stocks. Not only does this reduce the costs of holding buffer stocks, it also creates 'dynamic tensions' in the production process as a result of the all-pervading sense of crisis that accompanies interruptions in supply. Furthermore, the introduction of a zero-defects policy led to the responsibility for quality control being placed in the hands of shop-floor workers. This in turn challenged the conventional Taylorist and Fordist principles of mass production, in which tasks are broken down into their components and are undertaken by specialised workers, while the overall functions of control and coordination become the responsibility of functionaries further up the hierarchy. While Japanese factories remained hierarchically structured, there was an increasing call for 'flexibility' with regard to the tasks performed at lower levels of the hierarchy. This example is important in itself, and has served to challenge many aspects of the western 'technological paradigm'—a challenge backed up by the dramatic competitiveness of Japanese goods in western markets. However, for present purposes, the main significance of this example is that it serves to highlight the importance of selectivity in ways of thinking about, or structuring, technological knowledge. The implication is that knowledge is itself a flexible resource which, while always selectively structured, can also under some circumstances be selectively *re*structured. In turn this line of reasoning raises many other questions (which, however, will not be pursued here) that need to be examined if the role of technological knowledge in economic change is to be better understood.

(b). The firm and its environment: a microscopic/macroscopic analysis
Firms are influenced by their environmental conditions. In order to understand the interactions between firms and their environment, it is necessary to move away from the single-minded emphasis on market prices (noted in the quotation above from McNulty, and stressed in conventional micro-economics). While market prices certainly are important, and while changes in relative prices are a means by which information is conveyed to firms (as rigorously analysed in microeconomics), there are other factors that must be incorporated into an analysis of the interactions between the firm and its environment.

For example, the present survey has emphasised the importance of non-market-mediated flows of information in analysing the process of technical change. For instance, imitation plays a crucial role in many industries in less developed countries. On the basis of information acquired through a number of possible channels, firms in these countries may be able to adapt to change by copying the products and perhaps even the processes of successful rivals in the same and other countries. Imitative behaviour plays a central role in the process of competition, yet such behaviour rests largely on non-market-mediated flows of information. This is an area in which both theoretical and empirical work is required in order better to understand the processes at work.

Different forms of inter-firms collaboration also should be more closely studied. One example is the relationship between firms and their subcontractors which, it is increasingly being realised, is extremely important. It involves far more than the arm's length and price-based market interaction as conceived by neoclassical economics. The recent literature in this area contains significant contributions which have substantially improved our understanding of the factors involved. For example, Williamson (1975) has stressed the importance of the limitations on information and the corresponding possibility of opportunism. Dore (1983) has emphasised the importance of what he refers to as 'obligational contracting' which is a specific form of market relationship involving longer-term mutual obligation and trust, as opposed to the 'auction contract' as usually conceived in neoclassical economics, whereby contracts are continually changed in response to the price and quality conditions offered by sellers. Dore argues that while auction contracting may optimise static allocative efficiency, it does not necessarily maximise longer-term dynamic and X-efficiences which may, over time, be more important than static factors as a determinant of the buying firm's profitability. For Dore, the Japanese example is a particularly dramatic indication of this, although other examples are also to be found (e.g. IBM, Marks and Spencer). Further investigation is needed on the forms and efficiency of these types of relationship in less developed countries which, involving as they do an important degree of inter-firm coordination, exist within the 'interstices' of the market/hierarchy divide.

Further research is needed on the way in which firms collaborate on the basis of their market and technological resources. These forms of collaboration once again transcend the markets and hierarchies distinction and include interactions involving licensing, joint marketing argrements and joint research contracts. Here a useful link may be made with much of the work that has been done on less developed countries involing, *inter alia*, an analysis of licensing agreements and the activities of multinational companies.

It has been possible here only to give a few examples of the forms of interaction between firm and environment. However, enough has been said to illustrate the importance of moving beyond the conventional stress on price-based market relationships in order to examine other forms of interaction.

(c). Changes in technological knowledge

Here there is a need to move away from the assumption that technological knowledge is costlessly available to all, and known with certainty, towards a perspective on knowledge which recognises that this knowledge is (a) unevenly distributed among the actors; (b) acquired only at a cost; (c) almost always incomplete, in the sense that any actor's knowledge-set is smaller than the total knowledge set in existence (cf. for example, Simon's (1958) concept of bounded rationality which emphasises the limitations on the ability of the organisation to process information); (d) always to some extent implicit (for example, not all the information necessary is transferred in blueprints); (e) acquired, assimilated, stored and recalled in ways that require the operation of complex organisational practices with the result that these processes can never be assumed to occur automatically or with perfection; and (f) alway selectively structured (see the above discussion on the concept of technological paradigms).

The main implication of this is that the process of complementing the firm's stock of technological knowledge over time is highly complex. To understand this process it is necessary to take account of the firm's interventions, both in the external world as well as in its internal environment, to increase its knowledge stock. These interventions include, for example, search as an intelligence-gathering activity involving a set of organisational practices, licensing, joint research activities, experimentation with different processes and designs, reverse engineering, research and development, and learning. Further research is needed on the ways in which these activities add to and change the firm's stock of technological knowledge and on the organisational practices on which they are based. This is an important area for further work; the surface has hardly been scratched.

(d). Organisational change and resistance to change

Here the need is to move away from the neoclassical assumption that change is instantaneous and unproblematical (for example, the neoclassical analysis of the change in technique as a result of a change in relative factor prices, that is a move along a production function). A more adequate conceptualisation of the process of technical change must take account of the reality that change usually involves a degree of uncertainty, surprise, hesitancy, organisational ambivalence and, possibly, conflict.

In order to analyse the process of organisational change (which will usually be involved in the implementation of non-incremental technical change) account must be taken of the factors which induce such change. Here it seems worth distinguishing between pressures and incentives defined respectively as an actual or threatened decrease in profitability and the promise of an increase in profitability. The reason for distinguishing between them is that there may well be an asymmetrical organisational response involved. To the extent that organisations attach a higher significance weighting to an actual or threatened decrease in profitability than to the promise of an improvement (and there is some empirical evidence to suggest that this has at times been the case), organisational attention will be more quickly and intensely devoted to dealing with pressures than incentives. From the research point of view, this conceptual distinction shifts attention away from the *consequences* of variation in the firm's environment towards a concern with the *processes* by which change is achieved. This takes us back to the concepts of hierarchy introduced above, and raises further questions regarding possible sources of resistance to change, including both social factors – for example, conflict between different groups within the firm over the desirability of change; and technical factors – for example, rigidities in the capital stock as a result of the existence of dedicated machinery, etc.

The issues of organizational change and sources of resistance to change as related to processes of technical change open many areas for research that have not begun to be examined in the context of less developed countries.

(e). Diffusion and selection

Further research is also needed, incorporating many of the issues considered above, on the ways in which new technological knowledge is spread among firms both nationally and internationally and, in the process, further developed. This area of the international diffusion of technological knowledge is one where work has already begun but where more conceptual and empirical research is required. Further analysis is necessary on the ways in which the process of interaction between firms involves a selection process (akin to natural selection in the biological model) whereby some firms grow and expand on the basis of better-than-average performance, others decline and become extinct, and the overall concentration of capital and markets increases. Related work is needed on the way in which at the same time new firms (including small firms) find their 'niche' under suitable environmental conditions and either enter existing markets or establish new areas of economic activity (a recent notable example being the development of personal computers in the developed countries). The areas of diffusion and selection constitute a further rich field for research which, in addition to issues such as knowledge flows and organisational change considered above, raise other questions such as the functioning of capital markets.

(f). The role of the state

The role of the state in shaping technological knowledge in less developed countries is under-researched. Yet this role is extremely important, as seen, for example, in the state's influence on: the generation of new technological knowledge (for example, through the activities of state-owned or financed research institutions); the acquisition of technological knowledge by firms (for example, through state measures to accelerate the diffusion of technology); the mediation of the relationship between domestic and foreign firms (for example, through state intervention in technology-acquisition agreements; measures to insulate domestic firms from the effects of technological competition from abroad, for instance through restrictions on international trade; preferential purchase by the state from domestic firms etc,; the regulation of the environment within which firms interact (for example, the laws dealing with intellectual property rights; laws on competition); etc.

Clearly, as a result of activities such as these, the role of the state is central in the process of technical change in less developed countries and an analysis of this role is accordingly necessary in order to understand such change. Furthermore, there are important differences (between countries) in the pattern of state intervention in the area of technology. Compare, for example, the substantial influence exerted by the South Korean state over the acquisition and diffusion of technological knowledge (as documented in the survey) with the exceptionally liberal role of the Hong Kong or Singapore states in the same area. These differences need to be explained since they have an important bearing on national differences with regard to technology. Here too a combination of empirical and theoretical work is required.

CONCLUSION

It has been possible here only to point to some of the directions for future research. One clear implication is that in many instances a fundamental break with past modes of thought is required and new conceptualisations need to be developed. While this task is daunting since it means moving into the relatively unknown, the rupture with the conceptual past also opens up rich new areas for cultivation. In any event, if the aim is to understand better the processes of technical and productivity change, and therefore the process of economic change more generally, this challenge *must* be accepted for the simple reason that existing conceptualisations have not proved adequate to the task.

Notes

1. For an attempt to relate the experiences of the more industrialised Third World countries to African countries at lower levels of industrialisation and technology see some of the studies in Fransman and King (1984).
2. This section draws on excellent reviews by Stewart (1979), Cooper (1980), Cooper and Hoffman (1981), Lall (1982a: Part Three) and Dahlman and Westphal (1982, 1983).
3. John Enos has argued convincingly that this may be a simplistic and highly misleading way of viewing the transfer process in most Third World countries. On the buyer's side it is necessary to distinguish private buyers from bureaucrats whose motives may be complex and quite different from one country to another. See Enos (1982). For an application of games theory in order to analyse this situation see Enos (1984).
4. 'Knowledge' in this context should be broadly defined to include social circumstances. For an elaboration see Fransman (1984: 11-14).
5. Major studies of choice of technique have been carried out by a number of institutions. These include the David Livingstone Institute of Overseas Development, University of Strathclyde, Glasgow; the Economic Growth Center at Yale University; and the International Labour Organization's World Employment Programme (see, for example Bhalla (1981)). Given the practical difficulties involved in calculating appropriate shadow prices, many of the studies have used market prices together with sensitivity analysis. Some studies have calculated (private) unit costs at a point in time for the alternative techniques (see, for

example, Cooper, Kaplinsky, Bell and Satyarakwit (1981) and Cooper and Kaplinsky (1981)). Other studies, such as those from the David Livingstone Institute, have added a time dimension by estimating costs for the life of the project and then calculating total present value costs for the alternative technologies. These detailed case studies have provided a richness of detail which takes the study of choice of technique beyond the over-simplified two-factor input, constant product, model. One example of this is the David Livingstone study of choice of technique in bolt and nut manufacture by McBain and Uhlig (1982) which finds that the

most important conclusion ... is that the most critical factors determining the least-cost method of manufacture are overall market size and the composition of the market (in terms of the relative size of demand for products of different types, standards and dimensions). Differences in wage and productivity levels are only of secondary importance and easily swamped by the characteristics of the market (p. 4).

In order to disaggregate the inputs and take account of product differences, Stewart (for example, Stewart (1982b)) proposes a 'vector approach' which assumes that 'each technique consists of a set of characteristics, as does each product' (p. 5). (See p. 7 for a matrix of characteristics included for techniques and products.) One of the most ambitious attempts has been undertaken by Rhee and Westphal (1977) who examine the choice between imported and locally-made looms for cotton textile weaving in South Korea using both private and social calculations. This study concluded that 'the indigenous semiautomatic technology is the socially optimal choice to produce fabrics of less than approximately 60 inches in width' (p. 228). It was found that at the time of the study (although this subsequently changed) government policies 'encouraging the use of imported technology simultaneously discriminate against domestic textile machinery manufacturers, thus inappropriately retarding the development of the domestic engineering industry'. Significantly, the study also took account of improvements in the semi-automatic technology (shuttle enlargement and feeler installation). 'This adaptation of the semiautomatic technology partly explains its continued superiority ... at much higher wages' (p. 231).

6. In practice it may at times be difficult to distinguish empirically between adapting, improving, and developing new products and processes.
7. See, for example, Kamien and Schwartz (1982: 49–51).
8. This section draws strongly on the various writings of Nelson, Winter and Rosenberg.
9. For more detailed studies of the effects of social relations on technical change and productivity see Lazonick (1979, 1981), Bruland (1982) and Gordon, Bowles and Weisskopf (1983a and b)
10. An earlier classic in this area is Dore (1973).
11. Knowledge will always be to some extent firm-specific. However, this tendency will be increased by laws granting property rights over knowledge.
12. This quotation comes in a discussion of Marx where Schumpeter states that 'Marx saw this process of industrial change more clearly and he realized its pivotal importance more fully than any other economist of his time (p. 32).
13. For studies of similar processes in the case of steel production in Latin America see Dahlman and Fonseca (1978) and Maxwell (1977, 1982).
14. For some recent models of diffusion which incorporate both the demand and the supply sides see Metcalfe (1982) and Metcalfe and Gibbons (1983).
15. See Elster (1983: 67).
16. See Cross (1982). The main point of this discussion is that

The Duhem–Quine thesis ... states that it is not possible to falsify simple hypotheses because it is invariably conjunctions of hypotheses which are being tested. Thus if a particular hypothesis is found to be in conflict with some piece of empirical evidence all that we can say is that the conjunction of the particular hypothesis with a set of auxiliary hypotheses is false. We can never be sure that it is not one or more of the auxiliary hypotheses which is responsible for the anomolous empirical evidence, rather than the particular hypothesis in which we are most interested .... Following the logic of the Duhem–Quine thesis we are obliged to conduct our appraisal at the level of groupings of hypotheses, that is to appraise any target hypothesis *in conjunction with* its supportive auxiliary hypotheses (p. 320).

A large part of the problem, of course, lies in identifying the supportive auxiliary hypothesis. Cross discusses these in the case of the stability of the demand for money hypothesis (p. 324). In the present case of technical change the point is that we need to make a priori assumptions about the causal mechanisms involved in such change in order to be able to identify the relevant supportive auxiliary hypotheses. However, as noted in the text, we presently lack an understanding of these mechanisms.

17. This section is largely based on the introduction to Fransman (1986).

18. In terms of the Harrod–Domar formulation, capital-saving technical change increases economic growth by increasing the productivity of capital, that is, the output–capital ratio.

19. See Chudnovsky, Nagao and Jacobsson (1984) for an excellent discussion of the characteristics of the capital goods sector.

20. In the same article Rosenberg states: 'the common observation is not so much that technical change in underdeveloped countries has any particular sort of bias, but rather that it is entirely or virtually non-existent' (p. 142).

21. However, see Erber (1984) for the argument that incremental technological change 'is inherent in the dependent relationship' as analysed in dependency theory and that the fundamental technological constraint in Third World countries like Brazil enters at the level of basic design.

22. See Brenner (1977) for an interesting account of the reasoning behind Marx's assertion that technological innovation is inherent in the capitalist mode of production. See also Mackenzie (1984).

23. Similar ideas have been expressed by others such as Rosenberg (1976, 1982).

24. It is worth recording here Little's (1982) 'reconstituted' definition of neoclassical economics:

Neoclassical economics can ... be described as a paradigm that tells one to investigate markets and prices, perhaps expecting them often to work well, but also to be on the watch for abberations and ways of correcting them. Perhaps the single best touchstone is a concern for prices and their role. (pp. 25–6)

The problem, however, in connection with technology is that we have seen above particularly in section 2 where Arrow's work is discussed that there are many reasons to expect that technology markets will perform less than adequately. Accordingly, it has widely come to be accepted that state intervention is not only justifiable in this area but necessary if a successful transfer of foreign technology and local development of technological capability is to occur. This question will be pursued below in connection with infant industries and state intervention. Furthermore, an understanding of technical change, as emphasised in this survey, requires that we go beyond an analysis only of markets and prices.

25. For a helpful discussion, see Freeman, Clark and Soete (1982: Chapter 2)
26. See, *inter alia*, some of the work of Katz, Lall, Stewart, Cooper, Westphal, Dahlman and Teitel all of which, to a greater or lesser extent, shows signs of 'neo-Schumpeterian' influence.
27. For a detailed study of CNC machine tools in Taiwan see Fransman (forthcoming).
28. For an attempt to formalise this relationship see Metcalfe (1982). See also Metcalfe and Soete (1983).
29. The *ex ante* ambiguity in Japan is suggested by the remarks of the President of the Bank of Japan in 1950 that 'Promotion of exports should be attained on the principle of industrial specialization. For instance, efforts to foster (the) local automobile industry are a sheer nonsense'. (quoted in Bell, 1982: 17). For an account of some of the intra-bureaucratic conflicts that occurred in Japan in the 1950s and 1960s, including some of the disagreements between the state financial institutions and the MITI, see Johnson (1982).
30. 'Depth' of knowledge may be defined in terms of the cost of acquiring the knowledge. See section 3 above.
31. As our earlier comments on the relationship between science and technology imply, the view that sees causation running exclusively from basic science to applied technological research to production engineering is misleading. Causal links also run in the opposite direction with problems 'thrown up' in production leading to technological research and even in some cases to basic science. In the case of Japan Dore (1983) notes that:

> most leading firms were still, in the early 1970s, (very sensibly) devoting more effort to world technology reconnaissance than to their own original research, and the nontechnologist managers, economists and officials who create 'the consensus' saw Japan as primarily a consumer, rather than a producer, of new technology .... In the early 1970s most Japanese opinion

makers would have uneasily accepted the 'good imitators and adaptors, but no originality' image of Japan which prevailed in the rest of the world. By the late 1970s the cliché was 'a proven capability for originality in the development of commercial products out of basic research ideas; a poor record *as yet* in basic research itself'. And with that diagnostic cliché went another, prescriptive one: we must give more attention to basic research (p. 7).

32. As far as the present reviewer is aware these doubts have never been systematically examined in the case of Third World countries, particularly the Asian newly-industrialised countries, although there are no doubt numerous technology-related circumstances that are unique in Japan. Both Taiwan and Korea appear to be consciously attempting to emulate the Japanese experience, although it has been suggested here that thus far, they have been pursuing 'technology following' rather than 'catch up' policies. Dore (1984) and Ranis (1984) have both argued that Japanese-type 'international search and learn' activities are highly relevant to Third World countries.

33. The classical case is, of course, John Stuart Mill's *Principles of Political Economy*, Book V, Chapter 10 (1848).

34. For an elaboration of these and other related arguments see Fransman (1984a).

35. Krueger notes that:

    it is impossible for any researcher to estimate the value, which must have been considerable (in the South Korean case), of the informal incentives which the government provided to exporters .... This included the attention of the highest officials to exporters' difficulties; the somewhat more lenient persual of tax returns than happened to other businesses; the more rapid expedition of paperwork and government formalities .... No one has yet devised a means of estimating the importance of these types of considerations, but it cannot be doubted that they affected the relative profitability of exporting contrasted with production for the domestic market. (Krueger, 1981: 215)

    For further details on similar activities by the 'strong state' in South Korea see Jones and Sakong (1980).

36. A project entitled 'Productivity Change in Infant Industries' is currently being undertaken by M. Nishimizu and J.M. Page at the World Bank.

37. The consequences for performance of creating differential incentives by selectively promoting industries, as discussed earlier by Westphal, must be distinguished from the consequences of exporting. Here we refer to the latter.
38. This requirement will clearly limit the number of industries which have export-potential.
39. Morishima (1982) argues that the protection during the Tokugawa period in Japan which lasted for about 250 years until the late nineteenth century was necessary for the survival of industry during the more open Meiji period.
40. In the 1930s, however, the export ratio in Japan was substantially higher. I owe this point to Ron Dore.
41. A similar conclusion is to be found in Dahlman and Sercovich (1984: 39–40).
42. See *inter alia*, Lall (1979a, 1980a, 1982a, 1984a), Westphal, Rhee, Kim and Amsden (1984), and Dahlman and Sercovich (1984). For related studies on the phenomenon of Third World multinationals see Kumar and McLeod (1981), Lall in colaboration with Chen, Katz, Kosacaff and Villela (1983) and Wells (1983).
43. Even in Hong Kong, perhaps the only serious candidate to be treated as an exception to the above statement, the state has begun to intervene to facilitate various forms of technical change. For some of the details see Fransman (1982a).
44. At least that available in English.
45. An important and most welcome exception is Dore's (1983) case study.
46. See Nelson (1982) for an interesting attempt to evaluate US technology policy via a number of case studies.
47. See also Ozaki (1972).
48. For an illuminating study of the modernisation of the steel industry in Japan see Lynn (1982).
49. While cost–benefit analysis might be useful as one of the tools available in investment planning, the point made here is that it is not extensively used in the Taiwan case.
50. This statement refers primarily to narrow economic objectives such as long-term economic growth. An important feature of many 'strong states' in newly-industrialising countries, a feature usually not commented upon in discussions of economic policy, has been the low priority accorded to 'human rights'. Similarly, 'strong states', including that of Japan, are not immune from national corruption scandals.

51. For a staunch defence of this approach see, for example, Lal (1983).
52. In the technology context see, for example, Nelson and Winter's critical discussion of welfare economics (1982: Chapter 15). See also Lall (1981a: Chapter 2).
53. This does not suggest that cost-benefit analysis is of no use. As mentioned elsewhere in this article, it will be useful particularly as a means of making explicit, and tracing the consequences of, the different assumptions relating to costs and benefits. However, in the case of decisions where future technical change is likely to be important, it is improbable that cost-benefit analysis will yield firm answers on which a concensus can be reached.
54. As Nelson and Winter (1982) note:

    If one takes seriously the assumption made in some 'rational expectations models'–that all individuals know all the public policy options and the consequences (perhaps state-contingent) of the choice of any one–it is hard to discern any role for policy analysis .... The policy-making problem is simply one of arriving at a Pareto-optimal agreement. (p. 379)
    Clearly, such assumptions are only valid in a world of perfect certainty.
55. See Elster (1983: 55–68).

Bibliography

*Allen, G. C. 1981, *The Japanese Economy*, London: Weidenfeld & Nicolson.

*Amsden, A., 1977, 'The Division of Labour is Limited by the Type of Market: The Case of The Taiwanese Machine Tool Industry', *World Development*, Vol. 5, No. 3, pp. 217–34.

*Amsden, A., 1981, 'Technology Exports from Taiwan', New York: Columbia University (mimeo).

*Amsden, A., forthcoming, 'The Rate of Growth of Demand and Technological Change', *Cambridge Journal of Economics*.

*Amsden, A. and L. Kim, 1982, 'Korea's Technology Exports and Acquisition of Technological Capability', Washington, DC: World Bank, Development Research Department (mimeo).

*Arrow, K., 1962a, 'Economic Welfare and the Allocation of Resources for Invention', in N. Rosenberg (ed.), *The Economics of Technological Change*, Harmondsworth: Penguin, 1971.

*Arrow, K. J., 1962b, 'The Economic Implications of Learning by Doing', *Review of Economic Studies*, Vol. 29, pp. 155–73.

*Balassa, B. and Associates, 1971, *The Structure of Protection in Developing Countries*, Baltimore: Johns Hopkins University Press for World Bank and IDB.

*Balassa, B. and Associates, 1982, *Development Strategies in Semi-Industrialised Countries*, Baltimore: Johns Hopkins University Press for World Bank.

*The asterisks indicate works referred to in the text. The other items on technology are included for information.

*Baranek, W. and G. Ranis, 1978, *Science and Technology and Economic Development*, New York: Praeger.

*Baranson, J., 1981, *North–South Technology Transfer: Financing and Institution Building*, Maryland: Lomond Publications.

*Barnes, B. and D. Edge (eds.), 1982, *Science in Context: Readings in the Sociology of Science*, Milton Keynes: Open University Press.

*Bell, M., 1979, 'The Exploitation of Indigenous Knowledge, or the Indigenous Exploitation of Knowledge: Whose Use of What for What?', *IDS Bulletin* (Sussex), Vol. 10, No. 2.

*Bell, M., 1982, 'Technical Change in Infant Industries: A Review of Empirical Evidence', Brighton: Science Policy Research Unit, University of Sussex (mimeo).

*Bell, M., Ross-Larson, B. and L. E. Westphal, 1983, 'The Cost and Benefit of Infant Industries', Washington, DC: World Bank (mimeo).

*Bell, M., Ross-Larson, B. and L.E. Westphal, 1984, 'Assessing the Performance of Infant Industries', *Journal of Development Economics*, Vol. 16, Nos. 1/2, Sept.– Oct., pp. 101–28.

*Bell, M., Scott-Kemmis, O. and W. Satyarakwit, 1982, 'Limited Learning in Infant Industry: A Case Study' in Stewart and James (1982).

Bergson, H., 1963 *Evolution Creatrice*, Editions du Centennaire, Paris: Presses Universitaires de France.

*Berlinski, J. *et al.*, 1982, 'Basic Issues Emerging from Recent Research on Technological Behaviour of Selected Latin American Metal-Working Plants', Buenos Aires: ECLA/IDB Research Program on Scientific and Technological Development in Latin America, Working Paper 56.

*Bhalla, A.S. (ed.), 1979, *Towards Global Action in Appropriate Technology*, Oxford: Pergamon Press.

*Bhalla, A.S. (ed.), 1981, *Technology and Employment in Industry*, Geneva: ILO.

Binswanger, H.P. and W.V. Ruttan, 1978, *Induced Innovation: Institutions and Development*, Baltimore: Johns Hopkins University Press.

*Brenner, R., 1977, 'The Origins of Capitalist Development: A Critique of Neo-Smithian Marxism', *New Left Review*, No. 104, July–Aug., pp. 25–92.

*Bruland, T., 1982, 'Industrial Conflict as a Source of Technical Innovation: Three Cases', *Economy and Society*, Vol. 11, No. 2.

Canitrot, A., 1978, 'Method for Evaluating the Significance of

Macroeconomic Variables in the Analysis of Technology Incorporation Decisions', Buenos Aires: IDB/ECLA/UNDP Research Program on Science and Technology, Working Paper 12.

Chen, E.K.Y., 1979, *Hyper-Growth in Asian Economies: A Comparative Study of Hong Kong, Japan, Korea, Singapore and Taiwan*, London: Macmillan.

*Chudnovsky, D., Nagao, M., and S. Jacobsson, 1984, *Capital Goods Production in the Third World: An Economic Study of Technical Acquisition*, London: Frances Pinter.

*Chudnovsky, D., 1986, 'The Entry into the Design and Production of Complex Capital Goods: The Experiences of Brazil, India and South Korea', in Fransman (1986).

*Clark, N. and A. Parthasarathi, 1982, 'Science-based Industrialization in a Developing Country: The Case of the Indian Scientific Instruments Industry 1947–1968', *Modern Asian Studies*, Vol. 16.

*Cody, J., Hughes, H. and D. Wall (eds.), 1980, *Policies for Industrial Progress in Developing Countries*, London: Oxford University Press in Association with UNIDO and World Bank.

*Constant, E.W., 1980, 'A Model for Technological Change' in *The Origins of the Turbojet Revolution*, Baltimore: Johns Hopkins University Press.

*Cooper, C., 1973a, 'Science, Technology and Production in the Underdeveloped Countries: An Introduction' in Cooper (1973b).

*Cooper, C. (ed.), 1973b, *Science, Technology and Development: The Political Economy of Technical Advance in Underdeveloped Countries*, London: Frank Cass.

*Cooper, C., 1974a, 'Second-Hand Equipment in a Developing Country', *ILO*

*Cooper, C., 1974b, 'Science Policy and Technological Change in Underdeveloped Economies', *World Development*, Vol. 2, No. 3.

*Cooper, C., 1980, 'Policy Interventions for Technological Innovation in Developing Countries', Washington, DC: World Bank, Staff Working Paper No. 441.

*Cooper, C. and Kurt Hoffman, 1981, 'Transactions in Technology and Implications for Developing Countries', Brighton: Science Policy Research Unit and Institute of Development Studies at University of Sussex (mimeo).

*Cooper, C. and R. Kaplinsky, 1981, 'Second-Hand Equipment in Developing Countries: Jute Processing Machinery in Kenya', in Bhalla (1981).

*Cooper, C., Kaplinsky, R., Bell, R. and W. Satyarakwit, 1981,

'Choice of Techniques for Can Making in Kenya, Tanzania and Thailand' in Bhalla (1981).

*Corden, W.M., 1974, *Trade Policy and Economic Welfare*, Oxford: Oxford University Press.

*Corden, W.M., 1980, 'Trade Policies', in Cody, Hughes and Wall (1980).

*Corden, W.M., 1981, 'Comment', in Hong and Krause (1981).

*Cortez, M., 1978, 'Argentina: Technical Development and Technology Exports to LDCs', Washington, DC: Economics of Industry Division, World Bank.

*Crane, D., 1977, 'Technological Innovation in Developing Countries: A Review of the Literature', *Research Policy*, Vol. 6, pp. 374–95.

*Cross, R., 1982, 'The Duhem–Quine Thesis, Lakatos and the Appraisal of Theories in Macroeconomics', *Economic Journal*, Vol. 92, pp. 320–40.

*Dahlman, C. J., 1981, 'A Macroeconomic Approach to Technical Change: The Evolution of the Usiminas Steel Firms in Brazil', Yale University, doctoral dissertation (unpublished).

*Dahlman, C. J., 1982, 'Foreign Technology and Indigenous Technological Capability in Brazil', paper presented at the University of Edinburgh Workshop on Facilitating Indigenous Technological Capability, Edinburgh.

*Dahlman, C. J. and F.V. Fonseca, 1978, 'From Technological Dependence to Technological Development: The Case of the Usiminas Steel Plant in Brazil', Buenos Aires: IDB/ECLA/UNDP/DRC Regional Program of Studies on Scientific and Technical Development in Latin America, Working Paper 21.

*Dahlman, C. J. and F. Sercovich, 1984, 'Exports of Technology from Semi-Industrialized Economies', ms.; published as 'Exports of Technology from Semi-Industrial Economies and Local Technological Development', *Journal of Development Economics*, Vol. 16, Nos. 1/2, Sept.–Oct., pp. 63–99.

*Dahlman, C. J. and L. Westphal, 1982, 'Technological Effort in Industrial Development: A Survey' in Stewart and James (1982).

*Dahlman, C.J. and L. Westphal, 1983, 'The Transfer of Technology–Issues in the Acquisition of Technological Capability by Developing Countries', *Finance and Development*, Vol. 20, No. 4.

Datta-Chaudhuri, M. K., 1979, 'Industrialization and Foreign Trade: An Analysis Based on the Development Experiences of the Republic of Korea and the Phillipines', Bangkok: ILO-ARTEP,

Asian Employment Programme Working Paper.

Datta Mitra, J., 1979, 'The Capital Goods Sector in LDCs: A Case for State Intervention?', Washington, DC: World Bank, Staff Working Paper No. 343.

David, P.A., 1975, *Technical Change, Innovation and Economic Growth*, London: Cambridge University Press.

Desai, A.V., 1975, 'Research and Development in India', *Margin: Quarterly Journal of National Council of Applied Economic Research*, Vol. 7, No. 2.

Desai, A.V., 1980, 'The Origin and Direction of Industrial R & D in India', *Research Policy*, Vol. 9.

*Dore, R., 1973, *British Factory–Japanese Factory: The Origins of National Diversity Industrial Relations*, London: Allen & Unwin.

*Dore, R., 1983, *A Case Study of Technology Forecasting in Japan: The Next Generation Base Technologies Development Programme*, London: Technical Change Centre.

Dore, R.P., 1983, 'Goodwill and the Spirit of Market Capitalism', *The British Journal of Sociology*, Vol. XXXIV, No. 4, pp. 459–82.

*Dore, R., 1984, 'Technological Self-Reliance: Sturdy Ideal or Self-Serving Rhetoric', in Fransman and King (1984).

*Dosi, G., 1982, 'Technological Paradigms and Technological Trajectories: A Suggested Interpretation of the Determinants of Technological Change', *Research Policy*, Vol. 11, pp. 147–62.

*Elster, J., 1983, *Explaining Technical Change*, Cambridge: Cambridge University Press.

Enos, J. L., 1962, 'Invention and Innovation in the Petroleum Refining Industry', in *The Rate and Direction of Inventive Activity: Economic and Social Factors*, Princeton: Princeton University Press.

*Enos, J. L., 1982, 'The Choice of Technique vs. the Choice of Beneficiary: What the Third World Chooses', in Stewart and James (1982).

*Enos, J. L., 1984, 'Game Theoretic Approach to Choice of Technology in Developing Countries', Geneva: ILO, World Employment Programme.

Erber, F. S., 1978, 'Technological Development and State Intervention: A Study of the Brazilian Capital Goods Industry', University of Sussex, D. Phil. dissertation.

*Erber, F. S., 1984, 'Technological Dependence and Learning Revisited', Institute of Industrial Economics, University of Rio de Janeiro (mimeo).

Fajnzylber, F., 1979a, 'Mexico: Capital Goods Program. Conception, Content and Achievement', UNIDO Seminar on Strategies for Development of the Capital Goods Sector, Algiers.

Fajnzylber, F., 1979b, 'The Role of Technology in Planning the Capital Goods Industry', UNIDO Symposium on Science and Technology in Development Planning, Mexico.

Fei, J.C.H., 1977, *Technology in a Developing Country: The Case of Taiwan*, New Haven: Economic Growth Center, Yale University.

Fidel, J., Lucangeli, J. and P. Sheperd, 1978, 'The Argentine Cigarette Industry: Technological Profile and Behaviour', Buenos Aires: IDB/ECLA Research Program in Science and Technology, Working Paper 7.

*Findlay, R., 1981, 'Comment', in Hong and Krause (1981).

*Forsyth, D.J.C., McBain, N., and R.F. Solomon, 1982, 'Technical Rigidity and Appropriate Technology in Less Developed Countries', in Stewart and James (1982).

*Fransman, M., 1982a, 'Learning and the Capital Goods Sector Under Free Trade: The Case of Hong Kong', *World Development*, Vol. 10, No. 11.

*Fransman, M. (ed.), 1982b, *Industry and Accumulation in Africa*, London: Heinemann.

*Fransman, M., 1984a 'Explaining the Success of Asian NICs: Incentives and Technology', *IDS Bulletin* (Sussex), Vol. 15, No. 2, April.

Fransman, M., 1984b 'Promoting Technological Capability in the Capital Goods Sector: The Case of Singapore', *Research Policy*, Vol. 13, pp. 33–54.

Fransman, M., 1984c, 'Some Hypotheses Regarding Indigenous Technological Capability and the Case of Machine Production in Hong Kong', in Fransman and King (1984).

*Fransman, M., 1984d, 'Technological Capability in the Third World: An Overview', in Fransman and King (1984).

Fransman, M. and K. King (eds.), 1984, *Technological Capability in the Third World*, London: Macmillan.

*Fransman, M. (ed.), 1986, *Machinery and Economic Development*, London: Macmillan.

*Fransman, M., forthcoming, 'International Competitiveness, International Diffusion of Technology and the State: A Case Study from Taiwan and Japan', *World Development*.

*Freeman, C., 1974, *The Economics of Industrial Innovation*, Harmondsworth: Penguin.

*Freeman, C., Clark, J. and L. Soete, 1982, *Unemployment and Technical Innovation: A Study of Long Waves and Economic Development*, London: Frances Pinter.

*Gaude, J., 1981, 'Capital–Labour Substitution Possibilities: A Review of Empirical Evidence' in Bhalla (1981).

Ghatak, S., 1981, *Technology Transfer to Developing Countries: The Case of the Fertilizer Industry*, Greenwich, CT: Jai Press.

Ghymu, K.I., 1980, 'MNEs from the Third World', *Journal of International Business Studies*, Autumn.

*Gilfillan, S., 1935, *Inventing the Ship*, Chicago: Follet.

*Gordon, D. M., Bowles, S., and T. E. Weisskopf, 1983a, 'Hearts and Minds: A Social Model of Aggregate Productivity Growth in the United States, 1948–1979', *Brookings Papers on Economic Activity*, No. 1.

*Gordon, D. M., Bowles, S., and T. E. Weisskopf, 1983b, *Beyond the Wasteland: A Democratic Alternative to Economic Decline*, New York: Anchor Press.

Harvey, R. A., 1979, 'Learning in Production', *The Statistician*, Vol. 28, pp. 39–57.

*Herrera, A., 1973, 'Social Determinants of Science in Latin America: Explicit Science Policy and Implicit Science Policy', in Cooper (1973b).

*Hirschman, A. O., 1982, 'The Rise and Decline of Development Economics', in M. Gersovitz, C. F. Diaz-Alejandro, G. Ranis and M. Rosenzweig (eds.), *The Theory and Experience of Economic Development: Essays in Honour of Sir W. Arthur Lewis*, London: Allen & Unwin.

Hirschman, W. B., 1964, 'Profit from the Learning Curve', *Harvard Business Review*, Vol. 42.

*Hicks, J. R., 1932, *The Theory of Wages*, London: Macmillan.

*Hicks, J. R., 1965, *Capital and Growth*, Oxford: Oxford University Press.

*Hicks, J., 1981, 'The Mainspring of Economic Growth', *American Economic Review*, Vol. 71, No. 6, pp. 23–29.

*Hoffman, K., 1981, 'Third World Industrialization Strategies in a Restructuring World Economy: The Role of Technical Change and Innovation Policy', paper submitted to UNIDO Global and Conceptual Studies Branch (mimeo).

*Hoffman, K. and H. Rush, 1980, 'Microelectronics Industry and the Third World', *Futures*, Aug., pp. 289–301.

*Hollander, S., 1965, *The Sources of Increased Efficiency: A Study of Du Pont Rayon Plants*, Cambridge, MA: MIT Press.

Hong, W. and C. B. Krause, 1981, *Trade and Growth of the Advanced Developing Countries in the Pacific Basin: Papers and Proceedings of the Eleventh Pacific Trade and Development Conference*, Seoul: Korea Development Institute.

Hsia, R., 1979, 'Technological Change, Trade Promotion and Export-led Industrialization (with Reference to Hong Kong and South Korea)', Bangkok: ILO—ARTEP, Asian Employment Programme Working Paper WP11-2.

*Hughes, T.P., 1984, *Networks of Power: Electrification in Western Society 1880-1930*, Baltimore: Johns Hopkins University Press.

International Labour Organization, World Employment Programme, 1975, A. S. Bhalla (ed.), *Technology and Employment in Industry, A Case Study Approach*, Geneva.

Jacobsson, S., 1981a, 'Electronics and the Technology Gap – The Case of Numerically Controlled Machine Tools', Research Policy Institute, University of Lund.

Jacobsson, S., 1981b, 'Strategy Problems in the Production of Numerically Controlled Lathes in Argentina', paper from workshop on Comparative Methodology in Studies of Technical Change, Research Policy Institute, University of Lund.

*Jacobsson, S., 1984, 'Industrial Policy for the Machine Tool Industries of South Korea and Taiwan', *IDS Bulletin* (Sussex), Vol. 15, No. 2.

*James, J. and F. Stewart, 1982, 'New Products: A Discussion of the Welfare Effects of the Introduction of New Products in Developing Countries', in Stewart and James (1982).

*James, J., 1982, 'Product Standards in Developing Countries', in Stewart and James (1982).

*Johnson, C., 1982, *MITI and the Japanese Miracle: The Growth of Industrial Policy, 1925-1975*, Stanford: Stanford University Press.

*Jones, Leroy P. and I. L. Sakong, 1980, *Government, Business and Entrepreneurship in Economic Development: The Korean Case*, Cambridge, MA: Harvard University Press.

*Kaldor, N., 1957, 'A Model of Economic Growth', *Economic Journal*, Vol. 67, pp. 591-624.

Kamenentsky, M., 1976, 'Process Engineering and Process Industries in Argentina and Mexico', report of research funded by the Canadian International Development Research Center, Buenos Aires (mimeo).

*Kamien, M. I. and N. L. Schwartz, 1982, *Market Structure and Innovation*, Cambridge: Cambridge University Press (Cambridge

Surveys of Economic Literature).

Kamrany, N.M. *et al.*, 1976, 'Brazil: A Preliminary Analysis of the Machine Sector'. Cambridge, MA: Center for Policy Alternatives, MIT (mimeo).

Kaplinsky, R., 1982, *Computer Aided Design: Electronics, Comparative Advantage and Development*, London: Frances Pinter.

Kaplinsky, R., 1983, *Sugar Processing: The Development of a Third World Technology*, London: Intermediate Technology Publications.

Kaplinsky, R., 1984a, *Automation: The Technology and Society*, London: Longman.

Kaplinsky, R., 1984b, 'Changing Patterns of Industrial Location and International Competition: The Role of TNCs and the Impact of Microelectronics', New York: United Nations Centre on Transnational Corporations.

*Kaplinsky, R., 1984c, 'Trade in Technology – Who, What, Where and When?', in Fransman and King (1984).

Kaplinsky, R., forthcoming 'Microelectronics and the Onset of Systemofacture: Some Implications for Third World Industrialisation', *World Development*.

*Katz, J., 1978, 'Technological Change, Economic Development and Intra and Extra Regional Relations in Latin America', Buenos Aires: IDB/ECLA/UNDP/IDRC Regional Program of Studies on Scientific and Technological Development in Latin America, Working Paper 30.

Katz, J., 1980, 'Domestic Technology Generation in LDCs: A Review of Research Findings', Buenos Aires: IDB/ECLA Research Program in Science and Technology, Working Paper 35.

Katz, J., 1982a, 'A List of "Main Issues" from Recent Research on Science and Technology in the Framework of the IDB/ECLA/IDRC/UNDP Programme', Buenos Aires (mimeo).

Katz, J. (ed.), 1982b, *Technology Generation in Latin American Manufacturing Industries*, Oxford: Pergamon Press.

*Katz, J., 1984a 'Domestic Technological Innovations and Dynamic Comparative Advantages: Further Reflections on a Comparative Case Study Program', ms; published in *Journal of Development Economics*, Vol. 16, No. 1/2, Sept.–Oct., pp. 13–37.

*Katz, J., 1984b, 'Technological Innovation, Industrial Organisation and Comparative Advantages of Latin American Metal Work Industries' in Fransman and King (1984).

*Katz, J. and E. Ablin, 1979, 'From Infant Industry to Technology

Exports: The Argentine Experience in the International Sale of Industrial Plants and Engineering Works', Buenos Aires: IDB/ECLA Research Program in Science and Technology, Working Paper 14.

Katz, J., Gutkowski, M., Rodrigues, M. and G. Goity, 1978, 'Productivity Technology and Domestic Efforts in Research and Development', Buenos Aires: IDB/ECLA Research Program in Science and Technology, Working Paper 13.

*Kim, Linsu, 1980, 'Stages of Development of Industrial Technology in a Developing Country: A Model', *Research Policy*, Vol. 9, pp. 254–77.

*Krueger, A. O., 1978, *Foreign Trade Regimes and Economic Development: Liberalization Attempts and Consequences*, Cambridge, MA: Ballinger Press.

*Krueger, A.O., 1981, 'Export-led Industrial Growth Reconsidered', in Hong and Krause (1981).

*Kumar, K. and M. G. MacLeod (eds.), 1981, *Multinationals from Developing Countries*, Lexington, MA: Lexington Books.

*Kuhn, T. S., 1962, *The Structure of Scientific Revolutions*, New York: Oxford University Press.

*Lakatos, I., 1978, *The Methodology of Scientific Research Programmes: Philosophical Papers, Vol. 1*, Worral, J. and G. Currie (eds.), Cambridge: Cambridge University Press.

*Lakatos, I. and A. Musgrave (eds.), *Criticism and the Growth of Knowledge*, Cambridge: Cambridge University Press.

*Lal, D., 1983, *The Poverty of 'Development Economics'*, London: Institute of Economic Affairs.

*Lall, S., 1975, 'Is "Dependance" a Useful Concept in Analysing Underdevelopment?', *World Development*, Vol. 3, Nos. 11/12, pp. 799–810.

*Lall, S., 1979a 'Developing Countries as Exporters of Technology: A Preliminary Analysis', in H. Giersch (ed.), *International Economic Development and Resource Transfer*, Tubingen: J.C.B. Mohr.

*Lall, S., 1979b, 'Transnationals and the Third World: The R & D Factor', *Third World Quarterly*, Vol. 1, No. 3.

*Lall, S., 1980a, 'Developing Countries as Exporters of Industrial Technology', *Research Policy*, Vol. 9, pp. 24–52.

*Lall, S., 1980b, 'Offshore Assembly in Developing Countries', *National Westminster Bank Quarterly Review*, Aug., pp. 14–23.

*Lall, S., 1981a, *Developing Countries in the International Economy*, London: Macmillan.

*Lall, S., 1981b, 'Indian Technology Exports and Technological Development', *The Annals of the American Academy of Political and Social Science*, No. 458, Nov.

*Lall, S., 1982a, *Developing Countries as Exporters of Technology, A First Look at The Indian Experience*, London: Macmillan.

*Lall, S., 1982b, 'The Emergence of Third World Multinationals: Indian Joint Ventures Overseas', *World Development*, Vol. 10, No. 2, pp. 127–46.

*Lall, S., 1984a, 'Exports of Technology by Newly-Industrialising Countries: An Overview', ms.; published with revisions in *World Development*, Vol. 12, Nos. 5/6, pp. 471–80.

*Lall, S., 1984b, 'India's Technological Capacity: Effects of Trade, Industrial Science and Technology Policies' in Fransman and King (1984).

*Lall, S., in collaboration with E. Chen, J. Katz, B. Kosacoff, and A. Villela, 1983, *The New Multinationals: The Spread of Third World Enterprises*, Chichester: John Wiley & Sons (Wiley/IRM Series on Multinationals).

*Lazonick, W., 1979, 'Industrial Relations and Technical Change: The Case of the Self-Acting Mule', *Cambridge Journal of Economics*, Vol. 3, pp. 231–62.

*Lazonick, W., 1981, 'Production Relations, Labour Productivity, and Choice of Technique: British and U.S. Cotton Spinning', *Journal of Economic History*, Vol. XLI, No. 3, pp. 491–516.

Lecraw, D. J., 1977, 'Direct Investment by Firms from Less Developed Countries', *Oxford Economic Papers*, Vol. 29, No. 3.

Lecraw, D. J., 1981, 'Technological Activities of Less-Developed-Country Based Multinationals', *The Annals of the American Academy of Political and Social Sciences*, No. 458, Nov., pp. 151–62.

*Leff, N.H., 1968, *The Brazilian Capital Goods Industry: 1929–64*, Cambridge, MA: Harvard University Press.

*Lewis, W.A., 1957, 'International Competition in Manufacturers', *American Economic Review Papers and Proceedings*, Vol. 47, May.

*Lewis, W.A., 1984, 'The State of Development Theory', *American Economic Review*, Vol. 74, No. 1.

*Liebenstein, H., 1981, 'Microeconomics and X-Efficiency Theory: If There is no Crisis There Ought to Be' in D. Bell and I. Kristol (eds.), *The Crisis in Economic Theory*, New York: Basic Books.

Lim, L. and E.F. Pang, 1982a, 'Vertical Linkages and Multinational Enterprises in Developing Countries' *World*

Development, Vol. 10, No. 7, pp. 585–95.

Lim, L. and E.F. Pang, 1982b, *Technology Choice and Employment Creation: A Case Study of Three Multinational Enterprises in Singapore*, ERC Occasional Paper Series, No. 4, Singapore: Chopman, Publishers.

*Little, I.M.D., 1982, *Economic Development: Theory, Policy, and International Relations*, New York: Basic Books.

Little, I.M.D., 1979, 'The Experience and Causes of Rapid Labour-Intensive Development in Korea, Taiwan, Hong Kong and Singapore and the Possibility of Emulation', Bangkok: ILO-ARTEP.

Little, I.M.D. and J.A. Mirrlees, 1974, *Project Appraisal and Planning for Developing Countries*, London: Heinemann.

*Little, I., Scitovsky, T., and M. Scott, 1970, *Industry and Trade in Some Developing Countries*, Oxford: Oxford University Press.

*Lynn, L., 1982, *How Japan Innovates: A Comparison with the U.S. in the Case of Oxygen Steelmaking*, Boulder, CO: Westview Press.

*Mackenzie, D., 1984, 'Marx and the Machine', *Technology and Culture*, Vol. 25, pp. 473–502.

*Marx, K. and Engels, F., 1848, *The Communist Manifesto*, various editions.

*Mansfield, E. *et al.*, 1977, *The Production and Application of New Industrial Technology*, New York: W.W. Norton.

March, J.G. and H.A. Simon, 1958, *Organizations*, New York: Wiley.

Mason, R.H., 1980, 'A Comment on Professor Kojima's "Japanese Type versus American Type Technology Transfer" ', *Hitosubashi Journal of Economics* (Tokyo), Feb.

*Maxwell, P., 1977, 'Learning and Technical Change in the Steel Plant of Acindar S.A. in Rosario, Argentina', Buenos Aires: IDB/ECLA Research Program in Science and Technology.

*Maxwell, P., 1979, 'Implicit R & D Strategy and Investment-Linked R & D', Buenos Aires: IDB/ECLA Research Program in Science and Technology, Working Paper 23.

*Maxwell, P., 1982, 'Steel Plant Technological Development in Latin America – A Comparative Study of the Selection and Upgrading of Technology in Plants in Argentina, Brazil, Colombia, Mexico and Peru', Buenos Aires: IDB/ECLA Research Program on Scientific and Technological Development in Latin America, Working Paper 55.

*McBain, N. S. and Uhligh, S., 1982, *Choice of Technique in Bolt and Nut Manufacture*, Edinburgh: Scottish Academic Press.

McNulty, P.J., 1984, 'On the Nature and Theory of Economic Organization: The Role of the Firm Reconsidered', *History of Political Economy*, 16:2, pp. 233-53.

*Mensch, G., 1979, *Stalemate in Technology: Innovations Overcome the Depression*, New York: Ballinger Press.

*Metcalfe, J. S, 1982, 'On the Diffusion of Innovation and the Evolution of Technology', University of Manchester (mimeo).

Metcalfe, J. S. and M. Gibbons, 1983, 'Industrial Policy and the Evolution of Technology', University of Manchester (mimeo).

*Metcalfe, J. S. and L. Soete, 1983, 'Notes on the Evolution of Technology and International Competition', University of Manchester (mimeo).

*Mill, J. S., 1848, *Principles of Political Economy*, New York: Augustus M. Kelley.

Montano, A. E., 1981, 'Exports of Technology from the Private Chemical Industry of Mexico', Consultant's Report of a joint Inter-American Development Bank/World Bank research project, Washington, DC (mimeo).

Morley, S. A. and G. W. Smith, 1979, 'Adaptation by Foreign Firms to Labour Abundance in Brazil' in J. H. Street and D. D. James (eds.), *Technological Progress in Latin America: The Prospects of Overcoming Dependency*, Boulder, CO: Westview Press.

*Morishima, M., 1982, *Why has Japan 'Succeeded'? Western Technology and the Japanese Ethos*, Cambridge: Cambridge University Press.

Mytelka, L., 1978, 'Licensing and Technical Dependence in the Andean Pact', *World Development*, Vol. 6, No. 4, pp. 447-59.

*Nam, C. H., 1981, 'Trade and Industrial Policies and the Structure of Protection in Korea', in Hong and Krause (1981).

*Nelson, R. R., 1978, 'Innovation and Economic Development: Theoretical Retrospect and Prospect', *IDB/CEPAL Studies on Technology and Development in Latin America*, Buenos Aires.

Nelson, R. R., 1980, 'Production Sets, Technological Knowledge and R & D: Fragile and Overworked Constructs for Analysis of Productivity Growth', *American Economic Review, Papers and Proceedings*, Vol. 70, No. 2, pp. 60-71.

*Nelson, R. R., 1981, 'Research on Productivity Growth and Productivity Differences: Dead Ends and New Departures', *Journal of Economic Literature*, Vol. XIX, pp. 1029-64.

*Nelson, R. R. and R. N. Langlois, 1983, 'Industrial Innovation Policy: Lessons from American History', *Science*, Vol. 219, Feb.

*Nelson, R. R. and S. G. Winter, 1974, 'Neoclassical vs. Evolutionary Theories of Economic Growth: Critique and Prospectus', *Economic Journal*, Vol. 84, pp. 886–905.

Nelson, R. R. and S. G. Winter, 1975, 'Factor Price Changes and Factor Substitution in an Evolutionary Model', *Bell Journal of Economics*, pp. 466–86.

*Nelson, R. R. and S. G. Winter, 1977a, 'Dynamic Competition and Technical Progress', Chapter 3 in B. Balassa and R. Nelson (eds.), *Economic Progress, Private Values and Public Policy: Essays in Honour of William Fellner*, Amsterdam: North Holland.

Nelson, R. R. and S. G. Winter, 1977b, 'Simulation of Schumpeterian Competition', *American Economic Review*, Vol. 67, pp. 271–76.

*Nelson, R. R. and S. G. Winter, 1977c, 'In Search of a Useful Theory of Innovation', *Research Policy*, Vol. 6, pp. 36–76.

*Nelson, R. R. and S. G. Winter, 1978, 'Forces Generating and Limiting Concentration under Schumpeterian Competition', *The Bell Journal of Economics*, Vol. 9, No. 2, pp. 524–48.

*Nelson, R. R. and S. G. Winter, 1982, *An Evolutionary Theory of Economic Change*, Boston, MA: The Belknap Press of Harvard University Press.

Nelson, R. R., Winter, S. G. and H. C. Schuette, 1976, 'Technical Change in an Evolutionary Model', *Quarterly Journal of Economics*, Vol. 90, pp. 90–118.

*Nishimizu, M. and J. M. Page, 1982, 'Total Factor Productivity Growth, Technical Progress and Technical Efficiency Change: Dimensions of Productivity Change in Yugoslavia, 1965–78', *Economic Journal*, Vol. 92, pp. 920–36.

*Nishimizu, M. and S. Robinson, 1983, 'Trade Policies and Productivity Change in Semi-Industrialized Countries', Washington, DC: World Bank, Development Research Department, Report No. 52; also in *Journal of Development Economics*, Vol. 16, Nos. 1/2, Sept.–Oct., pp. 177–206.

O'Brien, P., 1980, 'Third World Industrial Enterprise: Export of Technology and Investment, *Economic and Political Weekly*, Vol. 15, Nos. 41–3, pp. 1831–43.

O'Brien, P., 1981, 'The Argentinian Experience in Export of Technology: Retrospect and Prospect', Vienna: UNIDO.

*OECD, 1972, *The Industrial Policy of Japan*, Paris: Organisation for Economic Co-operation and Development.

*Ozaki, R. S., 1972, *The Control of Imports and Foreign Capital in Japan*, New York: Praeger.

Ozawa, T., 1966, 'Imitation, Innovation and Trade: A Study of Foreign Licensing Operations in Japan', Columbia University, Ph. D. thesis.

Pack, H., 1981, 'Fostering the Capital Goods Sector in LDCs', *World Development*, Vol. 9, No. 3, pp. 227–50.

Pang, E. F. and L. Lim, 1977, *The Electronics Industry in Singapore, Structure, Technology and Linkages*, ERC Research Monograph Series No. 7, Singapore: Chopman Enterprises.

Parthasarathi, A., 1978, 'Electronics in Developing Countries: Issues in Transfer and Development of Technology', Geneva: UNCTAD.

*Patrick, H. and H. Rosovsky (eds.), 1976, *Asia's New Giant: How the Japanese Economy Works*, Washington, DC: The Brookings Institution.

Pearson, R., 1977, 'The Mexican Cement Industry: Technology Market Structure and Growth', Buenos Aires: IDB/ECLA/UNDP/IRDC Program on Science and Technology, Working Paper 11.

*Peck, M. J., and S. Tamura, 1976, 'Technology', in Patrick and Rosovsky (1976).

Rada, J., 1979, 'Microelectronics, Information Technology and its Effects on Developing Countries', paper prepared for the conference of socioeconomic problems and potentialities of the application of microelectronics at work, Netherlands, Sept.

Raju, M. K., 1979, 'Internationalization of Indian Business: Some Missing Links', *Eastern Economist*, 30 Nov., pp. 1066–75.

*Ranis, G., 1977, *Science, Technology and Development: A Retrospective View*, Economic Growth Center, Yale University.

Ranis, G., 1979, 'Appropriate Technology: Obstacles and Opportunities', in S. Rosenblatt, (ed.), *Technology and Economic Development: A Realistic Perspective*, Boulder, CO: Westview Press.

*Ranis, G., 1984, 'Determinants and Consequences of Indigenous Technological Activity', in Fransman and King (1984).

Ranis, G. et al., 1980, 'International and Domestic Determinants of LDC Technology Choice: Contrasting Agricultural and Industrial Experience', Economic Growth Center, Yale University.

Ranis, G. et al., 1981, 'Summary of Scientific Progress – PRA –80–18867', Economic Growth Center, Yale University.

*Rawski, T. G., 1980, *China's Transition to Industrialization: Producer Goods and Economic Development in the Twentieth Century*, Ann Arbor: University of Michigan Press.

*Rawski, T. G., 1978, 'Industrialization and Employment in the

People's Republic of China', Washington, DC: World Bank, Staff Working Paper No. 291.

*Rhee, Y. W. and L. Westphal, 1977, 'A Micro, Econometric Investigation of Choice and Technology', *Journal of Development Economics*, Vol. 4 (World Bank Reprint Series, No. 15).

*Rosovsky, H., 1972, 'What are the "Lessons" of Japanese Economic History?', in A. J. Youngson (ed.), *Economic Development in the Long Run*, New York: St. Martin's Press.

Ronstadt, R., 1977, *Research and Development Abroad by U.S. Multinationals*, New York: Praeger.

*Rosenberg, N., 1976, *Perspectives on Technology*, Cambridge: Cambridge University Press.

*Rosenberg, N., 1982, *Inside the Black Box: Technology and Economics*, Cambridge: Cambridge University Press.

*Ruttan, V., and Y. Hayami, 1971, *Agricultural Development*, Baltimore: Johns Hopkins University Press.

Sagasti, F., 1975, 'The ITINTEC System for Industrial Technology Policy in Peru', *World Development*, Vol. 3, Nos. 11/12, pp. 867–76.

Sagasti, F., 1980a, 'Science and Technology for Development: A Review of Schools of Thought on Science, Technology, Development and Technical Change', Ottawa: International Development Research Centre (STPI Module 1).

Sagasti, F., 1980b, 'Towards Endogenous Science and Technology for Another Development', *Technological Forecasting and Social Change*, Vol. 16, No. 4, pp. 321–30.

Sagasti, F., 1981, *Main Comparative Report of the Science and Technology Policy Instruments Project*, Ottawa: International Development Research Centre.

*Schmookler, J., 1966, *Invention and Economic Growth*, Cambridge, MA: Harvard University Press.

Schonberger, R. J., 1982, *Japanese Manufacturing Techniques: Nine Hidden Lessons in Simplicity*, New York: The Free Press.

*Schumpeter, J. A., 1966, *Capitalism, Socialism and Democracy*, London: Allen & Unwin.

*Sen, A., 1980, 'Labour and Technology', in Cody, Hughes and Wall (1980).

*Sen, A., 1983, 'The Profit Motive', *Lloyds Bank Review* No. 147, Jan.

Sercovich, F., 1978, 'Design Engineering and Endogenous Technical Change: A Microeconomic Approach based on the Experience of the Argentine Chemical and Petrochemical

Industries', Buenos Aires: IDB/ECLA/UNDP Research Program on Science and Technology, Working Paper 19.

Sercovitch, F., 1980, 'State-Owned Enterprises and Dynamic Comparative Advantages in the World Petrochemical Industry: The Case of Commodity Olefins in Brazil', Harvard Institute for International Development, Discussion Paper No. 97.

Sercovitch, F., 1981, 'Brazil as a Technology Exporter', Washington, DC: Inter-American Development Bank (mimeo).

*Soete, L., 1981, 'Technological Dependency: A Critical View', in D. Seers (ed.), *Dependency Theory: A Critical Assessment*, London: Frances Pinter.

*Soete, L., 1983, 'Long Waves, Technology and International Diffusion', Brighton: University of Sussex, Science Policy Research Unit (mimeo).

*Stewart, F., 1977, *Technology and Underdevelopment*, London: Macmillan.

*Stewart, F., 1979, *International Technology Transfer: Issues and Policy Options*, Washington, DC: World Bank, Staff Working Paper No. 344.

*Stewart, F., 1982a, 'Recent Theories of International Trade: Some Implications for the South', ms.; published in H. Keirzkowski (ed.), *International Trade and Monopolistic Competition*, Oxford: Oxford University Press, 1984.

Stewart, F., 1982b, 'A Note on Comparative Studies of Technical Change–Basic Concepts', in E. Baark (ed.), *Comparative Technological Change–Methodology and Theory*, Lund: Research Policy Institute, Occasional Report Series No. 5.

Stewart, F., 1982c, 'Industrialization, Technical Change and the International Division of Labour' in G. K. Helleiner (ed.), *For Good or Evil: Economic Theory and North–South Negotiations*, Toronto: University of Toronto Press.

*Stewart, F., 1983, 'Technical Change in the North: Some Implications for Southern Options', to be published in *Proceedings of I.E.A. Congress* (ed.), L. Passinetti, Madrid.

*Stewart, F., 1984, 'Technology: Major Issues for Policy in the 1980's', in R. Tandon (ed.) *A New World Order in the 1980s*, Wheelers Publishers.

*Stewart, F., and J. James (eds.), 1982, *The Economics of New Technology in Developing Countries*, London: Frances Pinter.

*Teitel, S., 1979, 'Notes on Technical Change Induced under Conditions of Protection'. Buenos Aires: IDB/ECLA/UNDP Research Program on Science and Technology, Working Paper 34.

*Teitel, S., 1981, 'Towards an Understanding of Technical Change in Semi-Industrial Countries', *Research Policy*, Vol. 10, No. 2.

*Teitel, S., 1984, 'Technology Creation in Semi-Industrial Economies, *Journal of Development Economics*, Vol. 6, Nos. 1/2, Sept.–Oct., pp. 39–61.

*Tyler, W.G., 1981, *The Brazilian Industrial Economy*, Lexington, MA: Lexington Books.

UNIDO, 1981, 'Technology Exports from Developing Countries–the Cases of Argentina and Portugal', Vienna: UNIDO/ICIS, March.

*UNIDO, 1979, *World Industry Since 1960: Progress and Prospects*, New York: United Nations.

*Usher, A., 1954, *A History of Mechanical Inventions*, 2nd edn., Boston, MA: Harvard University Press.

*Vaitsos, C. V., 1974, *Intercountry Income Distribution and Transnational Enterprises*, Oxford: Clarendon Press.

*Warren, B., 1980, *Imperialism: Pioneer of Capitalism*, London: New Left Books.

Watanabe, S., 1979, 'Technical Co-operation between Large and Small Firms in Philippine Automobile Industry', Geneva: ILO, World Employment Programme.

Watanabe, S., 1983, *Technology Marketing and Industrialization: Linkages between Large and Small Enterprises*, Delhi: Macmillan.

Wells, L. T., 1977, 'The Internationalization of Firms from Developing Countries', in T. Agmon, and C. P. Kindleberger (eds.), *Multinationals from Small Countries*, Cambridge, MA: MIT Press.

Wells, L. T., 1978, 'Foreign Investment from the Third World: The Experience of Chinese Firms from Hong Kong', *Columbia Journal of World Business*, Spring, pp. 39–49.

Wells, L.T., 1981, 'Foreign Investors from the Third World', in Kumar and MacLeod (1981).

Wells, L.T., 1983, *Third World Multinationals*, Cambridge, MA: MIT Press.

*Westphal, L. E., 1978a, 'Industrial Incentives in the Republic of China', Washington, DC: Economics of Industry Division, World Bank.

*Westphal, L. E., 1978b, 'Research on Appropriate Technology', *Industry and Development*, No.2, pp. 28–46.

*Westphal, L.E., 1981, 'Empirical Justification for Infant Industry Protection', Washington, DC: World Bank, Staff Working Paper No. 445.

*Westphal, L. E., and K. S. Kim, 1977, 'Industrial Policy and Development in Korea', Washington, DC: World Bank, Staff Working Paper No. 263.

*Westphal, L. E. and Y. W. Rhee, 1982, 'Korea's Revealed Comparative Advantage in Exports of Technology: An Initial Assessment', Washington, DC: World Bank (mimeo).

*Westphal, L. E., Rhee, Y. W. and G. Pursell, 1981, 'Korean Industrial Competence: Where it Came From', Washington, DC: World Bank, Staff Working Paper No. 469.

*Westphal, L. E., Rhee, Y. W., and G. Pursell, 1984, 'Sources of Technological Capability in South Korea', in Fransman and King (1984).

*Westphal, L. E., Rhee, Y. W., Kim, L. and A. H. Amsden, 1984, 'Republic of Korea', *World Development*, special issue on 'Exports of Technology by Newly-Industrializing Countries', Vol. 12, Nos. 5/6, pp. 505-33.

*White, L. J., 1978, 'The Evidence on Appropriate Factor Proportions for Manufacturing in Less Developed Countries', *Economic Development and Cultural Change*, Vol. 27, No. 1, Oct., pp. 27-59.

Williamson, O. E, 1975, *Markets and Hierarchies: Analysis and Anti-trust Implications*, New York: The Free Press.

World Bank, 1980, 'Brazil: Protection and Competitiveness of the Capital Goods Producing Industries', Washington, DC: Report No. 2488-BR.

Index